Grant Allen

The Duchess of Powysland

Vol. I

Grant Allen

The Duchess of Powysland
Vol. I

ISBN/EAN: 9783337040338

Printed in Europe, USA, Canada, Australia, Japan

Cover: Foto ©ninafisch / pixelio.de

More available books at **www.hansebooks.com**

THE

DUCHESS OF POWYSLAND

A Novel

BY

GRANT ALLEN

AUTHOR OF
'IN ALL SHADES,' 'THIS MORTAL COIL,' 'THE TENTS OF SHEM,'
'DUMARESQ'S DAUGHTER,' ETC.

IN THREE VOLUMES

VOL. I.

London
CHATTO & WINDUS, PICCADILLY
1892

CONTENTS OF VOL. I.

THE

DUCHESS OF POWYSLAND

CHAPTER I.

HIS FIRST BRIEF.

BASIL MACLAINE, ESQUIRE, of the Board of Trade, laid down the *World* with the air of a man who has refreshed his soul with the pleasures of good company. And, indeed, he had been revelling, at the cheap rate of sixpence, in the very highest society this realm affords. 'Great dance at the Simpsons' last night, I see,' he said, taking up his coffee-cup in his other hand; 'and Bertie Montgomery's lost a cool thousand again over that good-for-nothing two-year-old he entered for Ascot.'

'Who *are* the Simpsons?' his companion asked, by way of reply, helping himself as he spoke to a third large slice of toast, and looking up with an innocently frigid smile at Basil's handsome countenance.

Basil twisted his black moustache gingerly between finger and thumb in a preoccupied way as he answered offhand, with the easy, knowing air of the young man about town, 'Why, Lady Simpson's, of course. There's only one Lady Simpson in London, isn't there? Sir Theodore's wife, you know—the great gout and gravel doctor.'

'Oh, ah!' his companion replied, shutting his mouth very firmly. 'I don't know them.' Then, after a short pause, pointedly, 'Do you, Maclaine?'

The young man about town, thus seized at a disadvantage, took a large piece of kidney and a crisp bite of toast, both which esculents he thoroughly chewed with slow deliberateness (in a way that would have satisfied even Sir Theodore himself, that rigid advocate of complete mastication), before he answered, somewhat crestfallen, and with a forced smile, 'Well, I don't precisely *know* them, you know; not quite exactly what you may call *know* them; though I see them about sometimes, Harrison, at "At Homes," and so forth. But one likes to hear what's going on in the world, any way, of course, doesn't one?'

'Of course,' Douglas Harrison answered, with prompt acquiescence, glancing at his own hastily-read morning paper on the easy-chair close by. 'One likes to keep count of how the world wags. Seen that remarkable compromise in the tailors' strike yesterday, by the way? The men seem to have behaved extremely well, and they've got the extra half-hour they were fighting for at last out of those wretched sweaters.'

'Oh, indeed, have they?' Basil Maclaine echoed, half stifling a yawn. 'How very interesting!' It was his turn to shut his mouth tight with a snap now, and look profoundly unmoved. For you may take it as a general principle in life that whenever a man says to you, 'How very interesting!' he wishes to give you to understand, in the politest possible way, that the subject on which you are speaking bores him ineffably.

'Yes, they've got the half-hour at last,' his friend went on, musing. 'And Bertie Montgomery's thousand would have got it for them a week ago, and saved these poor souls, with their wives and children, seven long days and nights of suspense and misery. Bertie Montgomery's thousand! Gone on a racehorse! By the way,' he continued suddenly, pulling himself up short against a new-laid egg, 'who *is* Bertie Montgomery, now I come to think of it?'

The young man about town winced visibly. 'Why, Lord Adalbert Montgomery, don't you know,' he answered, with a testy little snort. 'Of course you've heard of him—the Duke of Powysland's younger brother.'

'And do you know *him*, too?' Harrison went on, smiling.

'No, I don't,' Basil Maclaine replied, cornered once more. 'What a fellow you are to nail a man down! I've only met him.'

'Where?'

The lover of good company paused and hesitated. 'At Goodwood,' he answered at last, after a short mental struggle.

'Then why the dickens do you call him Bertie?' his friend asked mercilessly. For Basil was quite right. If ever there was a man for getting you down and sitting firmly on top of your vanquished head, that man was certainly Douglas Harrison.

'Well, everybody calls him Bertie,' the young man about town remarked, on the defensive now. 'He's universally known as Bertie in Society.'

'But I'm not in Society,' Harrison interposed, with bland persistence.

'Well, then, hang it all! I'm sure *I'm* not,' Basil Maclaine answered, half nettled at his friend's quiet rebuffs. 'But I talk of people as I hear them talked of.'

'I don't think it's good form to talk of people one doesn't know by their Christian names—above all, in an abbreviated shape, especially when they happen to belong to the great and the mighty,' Harrison remarked decisively.

'You think it snobbish?'

'Well, I wouldn't have put such a hard name as that to it exactly, myself; but if you choose to suggest it, I think it might possibly be mistaken for snobbishness by a casual observer. It leads people to think you're pretending to an acquaintance that, as Kant would say, has no objective reality answering to it anywhere.'

Basil Maclaine went on chewing away at his kidney with most meritorious vigour. Sir Theodore would have voted him a gold Gladstone medal in open competition for the prize masticator. But he said nothing. The fact was, he had a profound respect for Douglas Harrison's opinion on all matters affecting the etiquette of the world; for, to Basil

Maclaine, human life envisaged itself as a sort of organized quadrille, which you must walk through decorously according to a fixed measure; and, being himself a well-to-do Birmingham tradesman's son, of very remote Scotch descent, he felt he was less acquainted with the steps in that polite gavotte than his friend Harrison, who was a gentleman born, the produce of an established country rectory. He had no great opinion of Harrison's views on subjects generally, to be sure, for Harrison was what he called eccentric. Basil thought him a trifle too sentimental and 'soft in the head,' as he himself would have phrased it, in his ideas at large; but in all matters pertaining to the established quadrille of human life he recognised at once that Harrison, so to speak, knew the figures. Was he not a scion of the beneficed clergy, nursed at Rugby, polished at Christ Church, and learned in all the learning of the Inner Temple? On any other question, therefore, the young man about town would have fought it out to the bitter end; but on a question of manners he knocked under on the nail, and solaced himself for his defeat by taking another stewed kidney.

'They're very well cooked,' he observed, with a critical air, ladling out a mushroom or two on to his plate at the same time. 'But then she always does cook well. She's a perfect treasure of a housekeeper, in her way, that girl is.'

'You don't mean to say you think she cooks them herself, though, do you?' Douglas Harrison exclaimed, with a face aghast at the bare thought of such desecration.

'Who? The girl?'

'What girl? Not Miss Figgins?'

Basil Maclaine laughed outright at his neighbour's outraged look. 'Well, I suppose she does,' he said, twirling his moustache once more, this time complacently. 'I've always taken it for granted. Anyhow, they're devilish well cooked, I know that much. If she doesn't stew them herself, she most efficiently superintends the subordinate who does them.'

'The stipendiary?'

'Yes, the stipendiary. Though I should think that creature far too stupid to do anything right, even under the most efficient supervision on earth—say Miss Figgins's.'

The two young men were breakfasting together, as was their wont, in their own hired house (or rather chambers), situated in that commodious and central thoroughfare known as Clandon Street, Bloomsbury. Their sitting-room, which they shared together, was neither large nor luxurious; but it was gracefully and tastefully furnished throughout, and daintily papered, in a way very rare indeed in London lodging-houses. When casual visitors observed to Basil Maclaine, with an approving smile, 'How awfully pretty your rooms are!' the young man about town used to draw himself up consciously, cast about him a careless eye, and drawl out in answer, 'Well, yes, they *are* pretty. One can do so much nowadays, you see, with very little money or even trouble if one only has a spark of native taste in the way of decorating.' But when they made the same remark to Douglas Harrison, that too candid young counsel learned in the law would answer enthusiastically, with a glance towards the door, 'Oh yes; aren't they just nice! Our landlady's such a clever, deft-handed body. She's a lady by nature, you know; with real instinctive artistic feeling, and she makes everything she touches look so bright and beautiful!'

Whence it may be inferred by a wise reader that in the struggle for existence, where the fittest survive, Mr. Basil Maclaine had been far better endowed with natural gifts for the fray by his progenitors and predecessors than that poor simple-minded young off-set of the beneficed clergy, Mr. Douglas Harrison, who gave others their due with such quixotic generosity.

After finishing his kidneys Maclaine rose

and looked at his watch—a bran-new gold hunter. 'Ha, a quarter past nine!' he said, with a put-upon air; 'I must be off at once. It's a terrific bore having to be down at the office at ten every morning. I wish to goodness I was a man of leisure like you, my dear fellow—nobody's beck and call to attend to but your own! That's the way for a man to live! Why on earth didn't Providence make *me* into a barrister, I wonder!'

Douglas Harrison smiled. 'Because it preferred to pitchfork you straight into a jolly good appointment at the Board of Trade,' he answered lightly. 'I only wish I had half your complaint and half your salary. The Board of Trade's a very good place indeed for a man to find himself in.'

'Well, it's gentlemanly, any way,' Maclaine observed, with philosophic resignation, going over to the mantelpiece in search of a match. 'There's no denying that. It's gentlemanly, any way. It gives one so many points of contact, you see, with the Very Best People.'

By which phrase Mr. Basil Maclaine always consistently designated the members of our aristocratic and official hierarchy.

'And, my dear fellow, it's a certainty; that's the great point about it,' Harrison answered with warmth. 'You've got your work in life cut out, and you've got your bread and cheese always safely provided for you. Whereas here am I, after all the money my poor governor's spent on me, still one of the great house of Briefless, hanging on by the skin of my teeth ineffectually from day to day, in the vain hope that the attorneys—on whose knees, like Greek gods, all promotion lies—will be graciously pleased one morning to wake up, of their goodness, and generously recognise my humble existence. Oh, it's sickening work, this waiting, and waiting, and waiting, and waiting, with nothing to come of it. It makes a man feel like a log in the world—of no use to himself and of no good to humanity. What am I, after all? A mere idle mouth at the feast of life—a drone in the hive—a purposeless existence.'

Maclaine lighted his cigar at the match he had struck, and puffed away contentedly. 'Rank socialism,' he retorted, blowing out a long column of thick white smoke with an epicure's enjoyment. 'Rank socialism, my dear fellow, every blessed word of it. I call you a jolly lucky dog myself: plenty of time to look about you and reflect; a good allowance from the dear old archdeacon meanwhile; the *entrée* of ever so many first-class houses; and in the end, some day, you'll get a splendid big case, and wake up next morning to find yourself famous. All you want's a fair start in life, a chance of being heard; that's where it is, Harrison. Once rise erect on your hind-legs in court and put them through their paces, and you'll astonish the judges, I'll bet you a sovereign.'

'I shall astonish myself a good deal more, then, I'm sure,' Harrison answered, laughing. 'I don't believe I've got the cheek to make a speech, if it came to the push. My law's all right, I admit, but it's my legs that are shaky. I should hum and haw, I know, with my knees trembling under me. Was that a knock at the door? Come in, Miss Figgins.'

The door opened, and Miss Figgins came in.

A casual observer would have noted first, as she glided into the room, that Miss Figgins was tall, dark, and extremely graceful. In another moment that hypothetical person would also have remarked that Miss Figgins's face belied her name, for instead of being in the democratic or tip-tilted style of beauty, it was clear-cut and regular, and very distinguished-looking. Not, to be sure, precisely what is called an aristocratic face; it had too much originality and boldness of outline about it for that; the pronounced chin and the calm, large eyes didn't mark so much the caste of Vere de Vere as the best outcome of the capable artisan type in our modern community. And, indeed, at a third glance, the casual observer in point would probably have concluded that capability was Miss Figgins's most characteristic attribute. She looked, in short, like a thoroughly competent person—competent to rule a household well or to deliberate seriously on the affairs of a nation.

Both young men assumed instinctively a more deferential attitude as Miss Figgins entered. Maclaine was leaning his elbow on the mantelshelf, in the act of departing, when the knock was heard. He let the elbow drop, and took his cigar from his mouth as Miss Figgins, with quiet dignity, answered the barrister's summons. Douglas Harrison, on the other hand, was seated, and he rose from his chair hurriedly, with a look as if half of shame that Miss Figgins should have to submit at all to such commonplace drudgery. But the girl herself, all unconscious of their action, walked up in a frank but stately way to the table whence he had just risen, and handed a packet and a note to the blushing barrister. 'A letter for you, Mr. Harrison,' she said, with a quiet smile playing on that still strong face of hers. 'The boy who brought it is waiting for an answer.'

Douglas Harrison turned it over with a look of blank astonishment. 'This is wonderful!' he exclaimed, thunderstruck; 'extraordinary! miraculous!'

'What is it?' Maclaine asked, putting his head on one side and looking past Miss Figgins.

Harrison gasped for breath. 'Why, it's a brief!' he cried faintly. 'A real live brief, legibly marked, in a good legal hand, "Mr. Douglas Harrison."'

'A brief!' Maclaine and the girl both echoed at once. And Miss Figgins, looking across at her lodger with those large brown eyes of hers, exclaimed quite naturally, 'Oh dear, Mr. Harrison, I *am* so glad of it!'

For a minute Harrison was too busy examining the impressive document to say anything more about it. Then he added, with a sigh of intense relief, 'Yes, it's really for me! Not a doubt of that. It's a criminal case—a burglar, Morton and Maule say in their private note; or, rather, a client accused of burglary. And they *do* remark he's one of the men the police have long been most anxious to catch, for he's considered almost the most expert thief in all London.'

'Then of course you won't defend him?' Miss Figgins put in promptly.

'Of course he *will*,' the civil servant rejoined with equal readiness. 'That's just what a barrister's for—to give every man, however bad, his even chance of equal justice.'

'And they want me to call upon him at his present address,' Harrison continued, reading, 'at his own request, as a particular favour.'

'It isn't *usual*, is it?' Basil Maclaine interposed, somewhat scandalized, what was usual being to him the supreme law of existence.

'No, it isn't exactly usual,' with a deprecating cough—'not the rule of the profession,' the barrister answered. 'But still, as a particular favour, you know, I don't see that there's any good reason against it. He's committed without bail, they say, and he specially desired that I, by name, should be retained to defend him.'

'Why this unaccountable popularity among expert burglars?' Maclaine put in, much amused. 'By Jove! I've got it! He must have heard you spouting those rank socialistic ideas of yours somewhere, Harrison, and he thought you'd be just the fellow to defend a man and a brother unjustly accused of what you may call practical or applied communism.'

'A burglar,' Harrison went on, rolling the words on his tongue. 'I suppose I must accept the brief as a matter of business, and go to see him. But I could have wished, I must confess, my first client had been something a little bit more respectable.'

'You ought to be the last man on earth to

admit that he isn't,' Maclaine went on, laughing. 'The perfect advocate believes implicitly in the bland and child-like innocence of his client—till he's proved to be guilty. But I can fancy the style of innocent you'll be called upon to defend. I see his portrait in my mind's eye—a square-headed gentleman with close-cropped hair, a rat-trap jaw, a broken nose rather wide at the wings, a pair of most expansive and expansible nostrils, a black eye, somewhat recently relieved by the application of raw beefsteak, and an engaging expression about his face of general leering blackguardism. If you pull him through, my dear fellow, your fortune's made. The mere look of the gentleman, probably, 'll be enough to condemn him in the minds of twelve intelligent and impartial fellow-countrymen.'

'Well, I must go at once,' Harrison cried, undeterred by this fancy sketch, and rushing off for his hat. 'They say their client desires an immediate interview.'

'I'm sorry it's a burglar,' Miss Figgins

said, with a little sigh, as the barrister, no longer briefless, left the room. 'I wish his first case had been anything but a burglary.'

Maclaine shut the door gently behind his retreating friend. 'Why so, Linda?' he asked, looking at her with a more inquiring glance.

The girl moved round to the other side of the table, and began taking up the breakfast things with perfect dignity. 'Because it's so unworthy of him,' she said quietly, after a short pause. But a little red spot burnt bright in the middle of her cheek—a little red spot not wholly of anger—as always happened, indeed, when Maclaine, left alone with her for a moment, dropped the Miss, and addressed her by her Christian name as Linda.

CHAPTER II.

THE HEAD OF THE PROFESSION.

It took Douglas Harrison only twenty minutes to call on the solicitors who had sent him the brief (where he aroused the amused attention of the clerks in the office by his deferential nervousness), and then to go round in a cab to Holloway Gaol, where, under present circumstances, his prospective client was most unfortunately detained on a magistrate's warrant. When he presented himself at the gates, however, breathless and excited, he asked so timidly whether he could see 'a man of the name of Arthur Roper' on legal business connected with his defence, and otherwise showed himself so obviously unaccustomed to similar errands of a professional character, that the authority in charge at the lodge—a portly gentleman with a braided coat and a powerful voice of considerable asperity—had evident doubts in his own mind for several seconds at a stretch as to whether in fact Arthur Roper's counsel was really and truly the person he represented himself to be. But in the end, after some demur and some exhibition of credentials in the shape of that priceless brief, the young barrister was permitted to pass the large iron portal without further parley; and, being handed over to the custody of a second gaol official, with a big bunch of stern-looking keys at his side, was quickly conducted through a long blank stone corridor to the man Arthur Roper's existing place of temporary residence.

At the cell door Harrison knocked tentatively. A voice from the other side answered, 'Come in!'—not in gruff and harsh tones, as counsel had imagined beforehand would almost certainly be the case, but with a gentlemanly and not altogether ungenial accent. Douglas Harrison waited while the official, smiling broadly at the needless knock, undid a ponderous bolt; then he entered, somewhat nervously, the narrow stone chamber where his first employer was lounging in enforced idleness.

Douglas was prepared to see a very desperate-looking and evil-faced person indeed, for Mr. Roper's solicitors had described Mr. Roper to him during their brief interview as probably the most cunning and daring burglar then at large in any part of London. He had pictured to himself his first client much as Maclaine had facetiously described him—the living image of that typical Bill Sikes, with whose supposed lineaments *Mr. Punch's* cartoons have made us all so familiar—a flat-nosed, brutal-jawed, low-browed ruffian. But when he saw instead a tall, slim, well-dressed, and almost gentlemanly person seated on the bed, who rose up politely and gracefully enough and bowed his welcome as counsel entered, Douglas Harrison drew back with unaffected surprise, and hardly touched the small white hand his client held out to him with engaging frankness.

'I—eh—I beg your pardon,' he stammered out apologetically. 'I think there must be some mistake somewhere. . . . I wished to see a person of the name of Arthur Roper.'

The tall, slim man bowed once more in gentlemanly acquiescence. '*My* name!' he answered proudly, producing a card from a little russia leather case in his pocket as he spoke. 'Mr. Arthur Roper.'

'Ye—es; Mr. Arthur Roper,' the barrister echoed, glancing at it, and automatically correcting himself. 'But—eh—I hope you'll excuse me. The names and briefs must have got unaccountably mixed up at wash somehow. I was told . . . my client . . . Mr. Roper . . . was committed here—you'll forgive my saying it, but it's in my brief—on a charge of burglary.'

The tall, slim man bowed a third time with

marked politeness, and a smile distorted his pallid countenance. 'Well, yes,' he answered, evidently much amused; 'you've put the right name to it. That's just precisely what I'm run in this time for.'

'But you're not a burglar?' Douglas Harrison cried, starting back in surprise.

Mr. Arthur Roper drew himself up to his full height of five feet eleven inches as he answered, with conscious pride, 'Well, don't let's give ugly names to any gentleman's calling; but I'm generally considered to stand, in my own line, at the head of the profession.'

'What profession?' the barrister asked, more astonished than amused at the man's cynical shamelessness.

'Cracking cribs,' his client replied, with an easy smile, and nodded his head sideways knowingly.

Douglas Harrison had time to notice now that Mr. Roper, though gentlemanly-looking and good-natured enough, as far as features went, had a sinister expression lurking in his small green eyes, and an ugly smile playing about the corner of his thick sensuous lips that seemed the perfect incarnation of unblushing cynicism. He remarked also, that though Mr. Roper's costume was not wholly lacking in neatness or fashionable cut, his collar and cuffs were a trifle grubby, and his general appearance didn't seem to betoken any besotted devotion to the matutinal tub. In fact, he looked like a shabby-genteel broken-down gentleman who has seen better days, and has thrown away his cleanliness and his honesty together.

'But you're not guilty of the charge on which you're now committed, of course?' Douglas Harrison put in hastily, feeling that as a matter of the dignity of the profession he must at least deceive himself into a feeble belief in his client's innocence on this occasion, at any rate.

'*Of* course not,' Mr. Roper echoed with a cunning smile, accompanied by a faint or almost imperceptible vibration of the left eyelid. 'It's a point of etiquette in the profession, you know, that *this* time, always, one's unjustly suspected.'

'Indeed,' Douglas Harrison interjected, hardly knowing what else he was called upon to say.

'Oh dear yes, it's a point of etiquette in the profession!' Mr. Roper went on, seating himself on the bed once more, with dangling legs, and motioning his legal adviser into the solitary rush-bottomed chair his apartment afforded; 'and as the head of the profession, I need hardly say, I'm naturally jealous of its etiquette, much as the Lord Chancellor might be, of course, in your own line of business. Still, it can't be denied that habitual criminals, as a cold world chooses to call us, often *are* wrongly suspected. Take my own luck, for instance. That's the case with me at present. They've run me in, don't you see, on a trumped-up charge. Though, to be sure,' and he paused rhetorically for a second, 'it *was* a most unfortunate circumstance, I must admit, that I happened to be found in the top attic, and with a sectional jemmy up my right sleeve.' Saying which, with another faint tremor of his left eyelid, Mr. Arthur Roper laughed again melodiously.

'A what?' the barrister inquired with a puzzled look.

'A sectional jemmy,' Mr. Roper responded cheerfully. 'A jemmy that takes to pieces, you know, like a telescope, and then fits together again. They're common objects of the country, of course, to people who live by relieving other people of superfluous property.'

'But how do you account for your being there, then, at all?' Douglas Harrison asked, drawing back a little uneasily from the man's hilarious merriment.

'How do I account for my being there?' Mr. Roper repeated. 'Why, how on earth should *I* know? That's counsel's business, to suggest something that accounts for that, isn't it?' He nursed his smooth-shaven chin with one hand reflectively. . . . 'Well, I suppose,' he went on, after a pause, 'I must have been actuated in my conduct by a misguided attachment for the under-housemaid, who slept in the next attic.' And Mr. Roper once more smiled audibly.

'Oh, indeed!' the barrister echoed a second time, more puzzled than ever.

'Well, no,' Mr. Roper corrected himself, growing suddenly more serious. 'You're new to this work, and I mustn't mislead you. I wouldn't really like it to be put down to that. Not for worlds would I seem to do anything to demean my character as a gentleman, and the head of my profession. If I was trying on the Don Juan trick at all, I hope I'd fly a step or two higher than a common kitchen wench. Or rather a step or two lower, since the under-housemaid occupies a room, no doubt, at the top of the stairs, while the daughter and heiress has her own fair bower in less airy heights on the second story. However, you know, this is *not* business. I'd better begin and tell you all I have to tell, first, from my own point of view—omitting incriminating facts, of course—and then you can decide what sort of a defence you think you'd better set up to cover it.'

'I don't want you to tell me anything—anything that would hamper me in my pleading on your case,' Harrison put in hastily, in a shamefaced way, for his conscience pricked him. 'Of course I can't defend you unless, as regards this particular charge at least, I have some reasonable ground for thinking you are or may be possibly innocent.'

'Oh, that's all right, my dear sir!' Mr. Roper replied, leaning back easily, and hugging one knee in his hand, laid across the other, while he eyed his counsel with a close and searching scrutiny. 'I wasn't born yesterday. I understand perfectly the ways of you lawyer fellows. Why, bless you, I was a solicitor's clerk myself before I took to the crib-cracking line; and I had a narrow squeak of going up to Oxford, too, and being called to the bar—missed it by a fluke in a scholarship examination; detected copying off the fellow next me. Oh yes, you may well look surprised, but I'm a gentleman born; and whatever other mistakes I may have made in my life, I hope I've done something at least in my time to raise the gentlemanly tone of the crib-cracking profession!'

'You don't mean to say so,' Harrison replied, hardly able to resist expressing his contempt and disgust at the fellow's hatefully brutal openness.

'Yes,' Mr. Roper went on, surveying the bare wall with a stony stare of æsthetic disapprobation, 'and I'll tell you how I came to think of asking Morton and Maule to give you this brief—an unknown man like you that nobody's ever heard of—when I might have taken the case to Montagu Williams, who's got me more than once out of incredible difficulties. But the fact is, I happened to drop in at the Forum the other evening.'

'You don't mean to say,' Douglas Harrison cried, 'that you attend our weekly debates at the Forum?'

'Oh, indeed I do!' the habitual criminal retorted cheerfully. 'I hope I shall never allow close attention to the duties of my profession entirely to kill out all intellectual interests—all lingering regard for the things of the mind—within me. . . . Besides,' he added, after a telling pause, 'I did a little business there, too, in a humble way. I found a few stray articles of precious metal lying about loose in gentlemen's pockets, and I endeavoured to give them a lesson in carefulness by—eh—but, there, no matter.'

'I'm afraid,' Harrison said, holding himself still farther aloof, and feeling that cherished first brief slipping faster and faster each moment from his grasp, 'if you persist in telling me so many unnecessary and unpleasant details I shall find it quite impossible to undertake this case for you.'

Mr. Roper smiled compassionately once

more. 'All right, governor,' he answered, with a tolerant wave of the hand. 'Now don't cut up rusty, just when a fellow's trying to do you a good turn. The fact is, I'm engaged in observing whether or not you're the man to conduct this case. Well, as I was telling you, I dropped in at the Forum one evening this week, and heard you make such a capital all-round, slap-up speech on the emancipation of women question, that I said to a friend of mine—a lady herself—when I went home that evening, "Bess," said I, "you mark my words—next time I'm run in, hanged if I don't employ that young fellow I heard talking at the Forum to-night to pull me through with it!"'

'I didn't know I was speaking before a possible client,' Harrison answered abashed, but endeavouring still to clutch hard at that brief that so trembled to elude him.

'Well, that's just what I said,' Mr. Roper went on encouragingly. 'I said it, and I meant it; and now I've done it. I'm a good-natured, kind-hearted sort of vagabond in my way, don't you see; and when I heard how much you had to say in favour of that ridiculous nonsense you were put up to defend, I thought to myself, "That's a clever young chap, by George! and a well-spoken young chap, who can make a good case out of the most blooming rubbish; and if only the attorneys would give him his chance, he'd be another Montagu Williams in his time, you bet, blow me tight if he wouldn't!"'

'I didn't think it ridiculous nonsense,' the young barrister put in honestly. 'I believed and meant every word I said about it.'

'Then the more fool you!' Mr. Roper retorted, with unflinching candour. 'However, that's neither here nor there as regards our present interview. We haven't met to-day to discuss the woman question, or the liquor question, or any other question that's agitating society. What we've got to do now is to prepare this defence against the charge of burglary. I asked to see you personally, instead of allowing my solicitors to state the case to you, though I know it's unprofessional, because the man who undertakes my defence has got to have his head screwed on the right way, and no mistake; and I wanted to make sure, by a personal interview, of the point of view you took about it. Whip out your brief then, Mr. Harrison, and we'll turn to business.'

Thus recalled to the actual task in hand, Douglas Harrison, with a sinking heart, laid out the paper as desired, and began to discuss the heads of the possible defence, and the witnesses set down in the brief whom he might call to prove innocence of intention. Mr. Roper listened with a languid interest. 'It'll be seven years, of course,' he said once, 'if the police can prove it; but it's worth going out of your way a little bit to advise these witnesses—to instruct them as to their evidence; for the fellows in the profession will consider my case is a gone coon, and if you were to get me a verdict, why, your fortune 'ud be made; you'd be the most popular criminal lawyer in all England the day after.'

'I'm afraid,' Douglas Harrison said, shrinking back once more, 'if you insist upon giving me such unpleasant hints I can't avoid the inference that you wish me to suggest to the witnesses what lies they must tell. Were you really concealed about the premises, or were you not—at 47, Brook Street—on the evening in question?'

'Well, there's that awkward fact about my hat,' Mr. Roper answered obliquely, going on with the case where he last let off. 'That'll have to be met and considered, of course. To anybody who didn't know my character well, now, the appearance of that hat might be open to misconstruction. I confess the arrangement of the interior was devilish awkward.'

'What arrangement of the interior?' Douglas Harrison asked with a long-drawn sigh, for he felt this case was really getting beyond his swallowing capacities.

'Well, you see,' the client responded with an easy smile, 'I'd cut the lining of my hat into a sort of mask with a pair of eye-holes, to turn down over the face, in case I should happen to be observed and followed, as I was out that evening on private business. The police have most unfortunately got the hat, and they'll put it in, of course, in evidence against me.'

'That's bad,' his counsel murmured, having nothing else to say on the subject.

'Yes, that's bad,' Mr. Roper assented carelessly, like one who recounts some petty escapade. 'But that's not the worst of it. There's another awkward fact we've got to face. I happened, as bad luck would have it, to be carrying in my hand a light wooden cane, or at least what looked like one; but when the police arrested me it turned out, to my immense surprise, to be solid steel, with a knob on the handle that would fell a man at a blow as easy as look at him.'

'But you must have known that by

the weight, surely!' Harrison exclaimed, appalled.

'Ah yes, one would have said so! But it was painted like wood, you know; exactly resembling a common thornstick. A most ingenious imitation! And what puts the police particularly upon their guard about the stick's this peculiar fact—that it's precisely similar to another steel stick with which that poor fellow, Sergeant Holmes—you remember the case; they gave him a public funeral—was nobbled at Finsbury.'

For some time past, Douglas Harrison's soul had been seething within him. But at those fateful words he rose and moved hastily to the door. He could contain himself no longer. The wretched creature's vile murderous hints were too much for his equanimity. He could never defend this offensive reptile.

Mr. Arthur Roper rose up, responsive, as he did, and confronted him in surprise.

'Where are you going?' he asked, as

Douglas Harrison stood with his hand on the door-knob, waiting for the warder, at the preconcerted signal, to come back and open it.

'I'm going to return my brief to Morton and Maule,' the barrister said resolutely.

Mr. Roper drew back as if overwhelmed with astonishment. 'Going to return your brief!' he cried. 'The very first brief you've ever had! Why, what in goodness's name are you going to do that for?'

Douglas Harrison looked at him with profound loathing. 'Because I won't make myself an instrument,' he said, 'to aid and abet in any way the turning loose once more upon outraged humanity of such a dangerous brute and cur as you are.'

Mr. Roper's face was a study to behold. 'Do you know,' he gasped out, half choking, 'that if you return this brief, after receiving instructions, and interviewing the client, and worming yourself into my confidence, no respectable solicitor in England will ever again employ you? Do you know that I'm the head of the profession in London, and could have brought you clients, if you managed my case well, every assize time regularly? Do you know that I'd as good as have made a millionaire of you? You're simply ruining your professional prospects. I meant to do you a good turn, and I was feeling my way to see what you were worth; but you're one of those absurd quixotic fools that won't be befriended. No solicitor in England will ever again send a guinea brief to you.'

Douglas Harrison jammed his hat firmly on his head, and stood with his hand on the door as the warder opened it. 'I don't care a pin for that,' he answered warmly. 'I could never sleep in peace another night in my bed if I persuaded a jury to turn such a man as you loose upon the world once more to rob and murder.'

'Then all I've got to say to you, sir,' Mr. Roper remarked, taking a parting shot at the foe as the cell door closed tight with a bang behind him, 'is, that you're no gentleman.

To worm yourself into a professional man's confidence, and then round upon him like that! Preposterous! Disgusting! You may take it from me, sir, that you're no gentleman.'

CHAPTER III.

TÊTE-À-TÊTE.

When Douglas Harrison left the rooms in Clandon Street that morning, he left Basil Maclaine in possession, with his elbow on the mantelpiece, in the very act of setting out for the office.

But as soon as Basil found himself alone there with Linda, he certainly displayed no remarkable alacrity in preparing to sally forth, as in duty bound, to the service of his country. On the contrary, he stood still, with his cigar pointing downward and his eyes following Linda all round the room in mute observance, as though annatto and jute and the Board of Trade had never existed at all in this United Kingdom. Imports and exports moved him not to budge. Since Linda entered, his zeal for red tape had diminished visibly.

As for Linda herself, she went on clearing away the breakfast things in spite of him in a most business-like manner, absolutely free from all trace of self-consciousness, and therefore from any silly coquettish airs and graces of the lodging-house order. She knew, indeed, that Basil Maclaine was eyeing her hard; but for the first two minutes or so she took no notice of his rapid glances. Then she looked up suddenly, and said in the most matter-of-fact tone possible, 'You'll be late for the office, Mr. Maclaine. You told Mr. Harrison you were going off three minutes ago.'

Basil took out his watch once more—that bran-new gold watch, with crest and monogram neatly engraved upon it: *whose* crest, heaven knows—as he answered quietly, 'I've got twenty-five more minutes to wait, Linda. Oh no, you needn't stare. That's a positive fact. I meant to walk it ; now I'll take a cab. A cab rattles you down in twenty minutes, easy.'

'Why have you changed your mind, then?' the girl asked, all trembling within, but outwardly calm, and turning her great brown eyes in full flood upon him.

'Because I don't often get such a chance as this, you know, my child,' the young man answered in a very soft voice, advancing a step towards her. Linda made no effort to retreat archly round the table, as most ill-bred young women would have done in her place, but stood her ground like a sentry, and looked him back in the face with perfect frankness. Anybody could see at half a glance that whatever her artificial position in life might be, well-grounded self-respect was Linda Figgins's leading characteristic.

'I've asked you before not to call me "my child,"' she said with quiet reserve. 'It surprises me very much you should go on doing it when I've told you it annoys me.'

'Linda,' the young man said, dropping at once his flippant manner, 'you know your will's law to me. I'll try never to say those words again if you don't like them. But they come up to my tongue all of themselves, somehow, whenever I'm not thinking.'

'I'd rather you *did* think, then,' the girl answered, moving away with a certain confident ease, and continuing her work. 'You'd please me far better by avoiding what I dislike, and by doing what I ask of you, than by saying such silly things as that my will's law to you.'

Basil Maclaine paused, and glanced at her admiringly. She was a confounded handsome girl, Linda; there was no denying it. And she had such a quiet knack of keeping her place and yet preserving her dignity. He didn't know how it was, but if she'd been a lady born, he could hardly have been more afraid of her, after all this time, than he was now with that London lodging-house young woman. Not that she repelled his advances exactly; on the contrary, he knew she rather liked them; but she insisted he should make them exactly as he would have made them—well, to one of his own equals. 'One of his own equals,' he thought grandiosely to himself; for Basil Maclaine, Esquire, of the Board of Trade, though neither particularly high-born nor particularly well-bred, had a very good opinion, after all, in a certain sort of way, in his own inmost soul, of his own importance.

'Harrison's here alone with you, often enough, half the day,' he went on after a pause, by way of saying something to hide his sheepishness; 'but *I* can hardly ever get you for five minutes to myself without his poking in his nose to hear what I'm talking about. This is jolly good news about this brief of his, though; if he gets work at the Bar, that'll take him out more in the day, thank goodness!'

The girl swept off the crumbs from the tablecloth with her brush as she answered, somewhat dubiously, 'Well, I'm not quite so sure of that myself. It's not exactly the sort of work I'd like to see Mr. Harrison doing. He's too good for such business. I don't want him to be mixed up with thieves and burglars.'

'Linda,' the civil servant exclaimed with a reproachful intonation, 'why on earth do you always talk to me so much about Harrison?'

'Because I like him so much,' Linda answered, looking up. 'He's so kind and good. I like him and admire him.'

Maclaine came round her side of the table once more. 'I believe,' he said, half piqued, 'you like him better than you do me!'

'In some ways I do,' the girl assented frankly.

'But not in others?'

Linda let her eyelids drop slightly with a natural movement. 'But not in others,' she repeated rather lower.

'*How* do you like him best, Linda?' the

young man asked, dropping his own voice in concert, and pressing his advantage.

Linda stood irresolute, with the crumb-brush poised idly and lightly in her hand. 'Well, it's hard to describe,' she said, looking up at the gas-lamp now. 'I admire and respect him for his simplicity and sturdiness and goodness, I fancy.'

'And you don't respect *me*?'

'No,' the girl answered decisively. 'I don't respect you at all, Mr. Maclaine. There's not so much to respect and admire in you, you know, as in Mr. Harrison.'

'But you *love* me, Linda?'

The girl drew back a pace, and her lips quivered. 'I never said so, Mr. Maclaine,' she answered, palpitating. 'But it isn't always the best men one loves most easily.'

'Why Mr. Maclaine?' the young man persisted, taking her hand in his, half unresisted. 'Why not Basil?'

Linda let that deft and capable hand of

hers lie unmoved for a second or two in his without reproof. Then she withdrew it hurriedly, and motioned him back with an imperious wave. 'You mustn't touch me,' she said quickly, in a tone of command. 'How often shall I have to tell you, Mr. Maclaine, that you mustn't touch me?'

'And how often shall I have to tell you, Linda,' the young man retorted, smiling, 'that you mustn't call me Mr. Maclaine, but must call me Basil?'

'That's quite a different matter,' the girl answered, drawing a deep sigh, and going on with her work once more in a most business-like manner, as one who sternly stifles a foolish fancy. 'I have a right to ask you not to touch me. My hand's my own. You have no right at all to ask me to call you Basil. You've no right, indeed, even to call me Linda—though I've spoken to you about that so often that I'm tired of speaking.'

'But you let Harrison call you Linda when

you're alone with him,' the young man pleaded.

'How do you know that?' the capable woman asked, looking up sharply.

'I didn't know it. I guessed it. But I know it now, anyhow. And if *he* calls you so, why shouldn't I, I'd like to know, if you please, Miss Figgins?'

'That's quite another matter,' Linda answered, folding up the tablecloth, the opposite end of which Maclaine, darting forward, instinctively held for her. 'He calls me so as a friend. You try to put it on a different footing.'

'Harrison's very fond of you, too,' the young man objected.

'I think he likes me,' Linda admitted, replacing the tablecloth in its accustomed drawer.

'Likes you!' Maclaine repeated. 'Why, Linda, what nonsense! Of course he likes you. He worships you. He adores you. How the dickens could he help it? Who on earth could live in the house with you for a week at a time and not fall over head and ears in love at once with you? You know yourself it's simply impossible. He likes you every bit as well as I do, and you know he does, perfectly. In other words, he's just simply mad for you.' And he tried once more, in spite of previous warnings, to take that smooth brown hand of hers in his by a rapid flank movement. It was one of those olive-brown hands more attractive by far than any mere dead white one.

'If you persist in doing what I ask you not to do,' Linda said severely, 'I shall have to go away and send up the stipendiary to wait upon you in future. I only come up now as a concession to friendship. If you won't allow me to do as I wish, I must withdraw altogether.'

Maclaine fell back yet again. 'Well, but, Linda,' he said, pleading, 'if Harrison's so fond of you, and you let him call you Linda, and he calls you so as a friend, why on earth should you put me on a different footing ?'

Linda lifted the tray and stood hesitating by the door for half a moment. 'You know very well why,' she answered at last, all tremulous.

'No, I don't,' Maclaine retorted. 'Do tell me, Linda.'

The girl faltered a second, with the tray just dexterously poised on one strong hand and wrist. 'Because . . . I don't love *him*,' she answered slowly.

'And you do love me ?' the young man cried in eager accents, his face lighting up as he spoke with genuine pleasure.

'I never said that,' the girl answered still lower. But her heart beat loud against the steels in her bodice as she uttered those words, and the tray trembled insecurely on its dexterously-adjusted balance.

What might have happened next, or what use of his vantage Basil Maclaine might have made, if a sudden chance hadn't intervened to checkmate him, heaven only knows. For as the young man and maiden stood there irresolute, facing one another with a bashful countenance, as is the way of those who have just arrived at an understanding on such subtle points, a man's voice from below broke the perfect stillness, through which they could almost hear their own hearts beat, with a repeated cry of 'Linda, Linda!'

The girl started, and moved quickly, but not as if flurried or surprised, to the sitting-room door. 'My brother's calling me,' she said. 'All right, Cecil. I'm coming in a moment. I'm only just clearing up the breakfast in the drawing-rooms.'

'Good-morning, Linda,' Basil Maclaine murmured in a low voice, picking up his hat and glancing carelessly at his cigar, which had gone dead out meanwhile. Then he looked across at her with a meaning look once more, and murmured a second time, in still softer accents, 'Good-morning, Linda,' with a long-drawn intonation on that forbidden Christian name.

'Good-morning—Mr.—Maclaine,' the girl answered slowly. And Basil Maclaine knew from the faint catch in her voice as she spoke those words that she had almost yielded for the first time in her life and called him Basil. Then she walked away from the room with the same erect carriage and firm step as ever to go down to her brother. As soon as she was gone, Basil Maclaine, consulting his watch languidly for the third time, and re-lighting his cigar, observed to himself as he strolled away towards the landing, 'She's a confounded fine girl, upon my soul! Linda is; and I really do believe, if it hadn't been for that nuisance of her brother's interrupting us, I should actually at last have got a kiss out of her this time.'

With which consolatory and self-flattering reflection of an end almost achieved, he drove off in an exceptionally good humour to the Board of Trade, admiring the twirl of his own moustache as he went in the little strip of mirror at the side of the handsome which the acute commercial instinct of the carriage-builder has conceded of late as a peace-offering to the genius of human vanity.

CHAPTER IV.

CROSS-PURPOSES.

Basil Maclaine and Douglas Harrison occupied the first-floor suite of rooms—technically known as 'the drawing-rooms'—in Miss Figgins's Furnished Apartments for Gentlemen in Clandon Street, Bloomsbury. The suite below—technically described as 'the parlours'—were filled by Linda herself and her brother Cecil. It was nothing short of grotesque, Douglas Harrison always felt, to address that queenly creature in her statuesque beauty by such a ridiculously plebeian name as Miss Figgins; but since Providence and her progenitors had so willed it, he consoled himself with the thought that in all probability before many years were out she would see cause to exchange it for another and more euphonious one. Meanwhile, he minimized the evil as far as possible by employing to her in private life her Christian name of Linda. He had first adventured such familiarity in fear and trembling as a tribute to friendship; but Linda's gracious permission to use the shorter mode of address was so frankly and readily conceded that he used it now, in spite of his native shyness, with perfect freedom.

'What were you doing so long upstairs, Linda?' her brother asked, when she went down to 'the parlours,' tray in hand, after clearing the breakfast-table.

Any other girl in her place would most likely have answered: 'Taking away the tea-things, Cecil.' But Linda's ways were not as other girls' ways—she was infinitely more independent and more transparent. 'Talking to Mr. Maclaine,' she replied truthfully.

'You talk a great deal too much to Mr.

Maclaine, in my opinion,' her brother said, half displeased.

'That's entirely a matter for my own consideration,' Linda answered, not haughtily, but with a quiet self-respect. 'My talking can only hurt myself; and we're nothing here, surely, if not individualist. What have you come back for so early, Cecil? Are you looking for anything?' For her brother had returned from the tube works in his working clothes, at a most unaccustomed hour, and, standing on a chair, was rummaging ineffectually among the tacks and screws of the toolbox in the corner cupboard.

'I can't find that magnesium wire,' the journeyman engineer replied curtly, without noticing his snub. 'There's a job on at the works just now I'm showing the foreman how to do, and I want an end of wire to light up the inside with a little. It's a ticklish piece of machinery for these rough fellows to attempt; it needs a quick, trained hand and plenty of light to do it.'

'The magnesium wire's precisely where you left it last, my dear boy,' his sister answered with provoking coolness, producing it, 'here in that coil you were working at yesterday. You're a first-rate mechanician, Cecil, you know, and a wonderful fellow for electric apparatus; but you must admit yourself you're not strong on tidiness. If you hadn't got *me* to clear up things behind you, I don't know how you'd ever get along with your models, anyhow.'

The engineer looked down with fraternal admiration into her great brown eyes. 'I don't want to flatter you up, Linda,' he said in a tone of profound conviction, taking the little roll of wire from her hands gingerly with his black, begrimed fingers; 'but I certainly don't know how I'd ever get along without you at all, in that or in anything. You're just the very helpfullest and most methodical woman I ever did come across.'

'"It was the best butter," said the March hare,' Linda quoted, laughing. 'Now, after all that, sir, what do you want me to do next for you ?'

Her brother smiled. 'Not such a bad shot,' he answered good-humouredly. 'Do copy that drawing of the crank attachment out on a clean sheet before I come home, there's a dear, good girl. Are you busy this morning ?'

'Not very,' Linda replied, glancing aside at the type-writer that stood idle in the corner. 'I've just got to help the stipendiary, as Mr. Harrison calls her, to make the beds and dust the rooms ; and then I've got to see about the pudding for dinner ; and then I shall finish type-writing that manuscript of Mr. Hubert's—it's got to go into the printer's to-night, you know, for Saturday's *Athenæum* —and after that, why, I shall be quite at leisure. I'll have time to copy out the crank before they're back in the evening, if nothing unforeseen interferes to prevent me. Anyhow, I'll do it for you to-night at latest.'

'That's right,' her brother exclaimed with a

grateful nod (for he wouldn't touch and stain her clean hands for worlds with his own labour-soiled fingers). 'You *are* a brick, Linda, and no mistake! You're worth any man a clear hundred a year. He'll be a lucky fellow, whoever gets you. Though what'll become of the models and things when you're married and done for, Heaven only knows. But there, my best comfort is, that the nicest girls never by any chance manage to get married.' And with that concise epitome of the philosophy of matrimony as his parting gift for his sister's consolation, the brisk young engineer dashed hastily through the hall, down the front-steps, and round the corner to the neighbouring tube works.

But Linda stepped briskly upstairs, all outward calm, to make the beds with Emma, the lodging-house factotum, whom they called the stipendiary, while within, her heart was full of Basil Maclaine and the easy, meaningless, captivating things he had said to her just before in the privacy of the drawing-rooms.

An hour or so later Douglas Harrison returned, somewhat dispirited, from his visit to the gaol. As soon as his footsteps fell dull on the stairs, Linda ran up, all inquiry, from the kitchen, where she was engaged in the manufacture of that pudding for dinner—her famous Mrs. Thorpe—and caught a glimpse of his back as he disappeared slowly and heavily towards the drawing-rooms. The very look of that back told her quick feminine eye at once all was not well, and she tried to slink away unperceived into the kitchen again. But Douglas had caught her light footfall upon the landing as she slunk off, and called over eagerly, 'Is that you, Miss Figgins?'

It was always 'Miss Figgins,' officially of course, within earshot of the stipendiary or his fellow-lodger.

'Yes, Mr. Harrison,' Linda answered, half returning and waiting on the step. 'I heard you come in, and I thought perhaps you might be in want of something.'

'I *am* in want of something—in fact, of sympathy,' the barrister said in a very low voice, catching Linda's bright eye over the edge of the banister. 'Are you very busy just now? Could you manage to spare me a tiny ten minutes?'

'Not very busy,' Linda answered, unfastening her kitchen apron and tripping upstairs yet again with untiring energy. 'You're disappointed, Mr. Harrison? The brief hasn't come off? You've found there's some hitch or other about defending the burglar?'

Douglas Harrison sank down into the easy-chair with the boneless collapse of a dispirited man, and told her in brief the strange story of his interview with the head of the profession. Linda, all sympathetic, stood with an official duster ostentatiously displayed in her pretty brown fingers, leaning against the mantelpiece in one of those graceful attitudes which came to her naturally.

As soon as Douglas had finished, she stepped over and took his hand quite unaffectedly in hers, as a sister might have taken it. 'It's a disappointment, of course, Mr. Harrison,' she said in a sweetly soothing voice, 'but I confess I'm not altogether sorry for it. It may have been foolish of me—I don't know the ways of lawyers—but I couldn't bear to think you should take up such a case. If you'd really taken it up, I should never quite have been reconciled to the desecration of your talents.'

'Then you think I did right, Linda?' the barrister asked anxiously, as one who attached great importance to her favourable opinion. 'You think it wasn't silly of me?'

'Of course you did right,' Linda answered with conviction. 'You did just as I should have expected of you. If you hadn't done so, I should have been quite disappointed in you.'

'No, you don't really mean that!' the young man cried, beaming.

'Yes I do,' Linda answered with grave seriousness. 'I expect a great deal from you, you know, and I always find my expectations fulfilled. You're a person one can depend upon.'

'Well, that *is* good of you, Linda!' the barrister answered, still holding her hand, unreproved, in his own, for Linda never attempted for one moment to withdraw it from Douglas Harrison. 'If *you* think I did right, that's more than enough for me. I attach so much importance always to your judgment, Linda.'

'Thank you,' the girl said simply; 'you're always very kind and good, Mr. Harrison.'

The young man paused, and stared for a moment at the empty grate. 'And yet,' he went on, in a dreamy sort of way that Linda knew well, 'it *was* a disappointment; I won't deny it. I almost hoped that if only I could once see my way clear in life there might be some chance, perhaps . . . that some day . . . hereafter——' He broke off suddenly, and looked with a timidly-inquiring glance into those great earnest eyes of hers.

Linda shook her head with unalterable decision. 'No, no, Mr. Harrison,' she said firmly. 'No more of that, you know. I thought we'd agreed that subject was never again to be re-opened between us. If you're going to talk so, I must run down to my work. And, indeed, I must run down to it now, in any case. I've such lots to do—the pudding to make for dinner, and Mr. Hubert's manuscript to copy for press, and a drawing to finish for to-night for my brother.'

Douglas Harrison jumped up, full of penitence, at once. 'And I've kept you here talking so long about this wretched brief,' he said, 'when you were wanted elsewhere! You, the prop of the house! the main corner-stone of the establishment! How dreadfully selfish of me! Can't I make up for it now by helping you in any way? Can't I—oh—can't I manage that manuscript of Hubert's, for example?'

Linda shook her head with a capable smile. 'Oh dear no!' she answered with true feminine contempt for the clumsy male fingers, 'that would never do. You can't work the type-writer half well enough for press yet. Your brother'd never give me another article to copy if I were to send it in all full of blunders. Besides, I shall have time if I go off at once.' And, with a nod and a smile, full of sisterly recognition, she ran off downstairs, leaving the drawing-rooms irradiated with a halo of glory by the bare memory of her presence for the once more briefless barrister.

'She's a jewel of a girl,' Douglas Harrison thought to himself as she retreated through the door. 'It does make me so happy when I've earned her approbation. But I wish she would only feel to me as she does to Maclaine. I don't know how it is, nothing that I can do ever seems to make her regard me as anything but a brother.'

It's often so with a certain sort of man.

They're so thoroughly good, and girls like them so much, that they never for one moment dream of falling in love with them.

That evening, when Basil Maclaine returned from the Board of Trade, he came in with an air of very conscious importance. Something that had happened to him during the day was evidently swelling his shirt-front to even more than its usual expansive dimensions. He was full of his grandeur. His waistcoat hardly held him. It was with difficulty he listened politely to Douglas Harrison's account of the burglar fiasco.

'The more fool you,' was the only comment he made when Douglas had finished his tale of discomfiture. Of course, you know what you've done for yourself now. You've knocked the bottom out of your own professional chances.' And as he spoke he produced quite carelessly from his pocket a very large envelope, which, nevertheless, bore some obvious and distinct relation to the high barometric condition of his personal spirits.

'What's that?' Douglas asked, with languid interest, as Basil pretended to lay it down like some unconsidered trifle.

'Oh, only an invitation,' Basil Maclaine replied, ostentatiously displaying the card at an illegible distance. 'Garden-party next Saturday. Very smart family, too, in their way. I angled for it hard, I can tell you; but Charlie Simmons pulled it off at last for me. I believe I'm getting into the swim, after all. I'm beginning to know some of the Very Best People.'

'Rich people, you mean. Well, I'm glad of that—as it seems to give you so much pleasure.'

'It's going to be an awfully swell affair,' Maclaine went on, ruminating. 'No end of titles.'

'Hubert and I are going out next Saturday as well,' Douglas Harrison murmured casually, as Basil fixed the pasteboard into the margin of the looking-glass in the little overmantel, with an affectionate glance at its printed inscription. 'Down Leatherhead way. A garden-party also.'

'Not at the Venables', of Hurst Croft?' the civil servant asked, with open eyes of wonder.

'Yes, at the Venables', of Hurst Croft. Is that your place, too? What a curious coincidence! Why, if I'd known you wanted to go there, Hubert would have got you an invitation at once without any angling. Miss Venables said they were rather hard up for men, I remember, and she asked if Hubert could hunt up some recruits for her from the Government offices.'

'You never mentioned it before,' Basil cried, rather crestfallen.

'Well, it didn't interest me,' his friend replied, looking wholly unconcerned. 'It's a bore having to run down all the way to Leatherhead just to put in an appearance at somebody else's garden-party.'

The civil servant stared at him mutely for a minute in blank astonishment. How strange a man should think so little of his splendid opportunities for associating himself with the Best People! 'Well, Miss Venables is an heiress, anyhow,' he went on, in a more subdued voice, for he felt himself sat upon. 'They tell me she's one of the very richest girls come out this season. She's a magnificent match. There can't be much harm, at any rate, in taking a pot-shot at her.'

'In taking what?' Douglas Harrison exclaimed aghast, for the whole point of view was one thoroughly alien to his honest nature.

'Taking a pot-shot at her,' Basil repeated, unabashed, pulling up his shirt-collar. 'Of course I know I haven't much chance of bringing down the game to my own gun, or even, if it comes to that, of winging her. Too many big swells with handles to their names are sure to be aiming at her from a point of vantage, and it isn't likely a commoner will pot the first prize of the season in the matrimonial handicap. Still, if there's anything good going in the market, one would like to feel, as a matter of justice to one's self, one was standing one's even chance to win it.'

'Maclaine!' his friend exclaimed in a tone of genuine disgust, 'I'm positively ashamed of you!'

'Why so, my dear fellow? All the Best People marry money nowadays. Look at the way our aristocracy are all going off to hunt for rich wives among the unspoilt preserves in America.'

'I didn't mean that only,' Douglas Harrison answered in a very grave tone, 'though that's bad enough in itself. But how can you talk of any other woman on earth when I know the way you've gone about to make poor Lin—Miss Figgins unhappy?'

'Miss Figgins!' the civil servant cried out, starting back in surprise. It was his turn to be virtuously indignant now. 'You don't mean to say, Harrison, you really think it possible I could ever in my wildest moment dream of *marrying* Miss Figgins!'

'I think she'd take you,' Harrison answered with a carefully-suppressed sigh, 'if you were to ask her properly. At any rate, it's not right of you, while you're going on so with her, to talk about taking pot-shots at any other woman.'

'*If* I were to ask properly!' Maclaine repeated with a profoundly scornful ring. 'If I were to give her the chance! If I were to cut my own nose off! Of course she'd take me. Of course she'd jump at it. But am I likely to ask her? He flung himself with an air of patient resignation into the long basketwork chair. 'Just like your aristocratic insolence!' he muttered to himself half angrily.

'My aristocratic insolence!' Douglas Harrison echoed with a puzzled expression of face. 'Why, what on earth do you mean by that, Basil?'

'Well, that's always the way with you

fellows who've got a cousin a baronet and an uncle a general,' Basil replied with warmth. 'You think there are no distinctions of rank at all outside your own particular class or caste. You think all the rest of us who don't happen to be born in your exalted sphere are at one universal dead-level of hopeless vulgarity. You think because my father's in business, while yours is in the Church, I can marry a common London lodging-house girl, whose parents were labourers, I suppose, and whose brother's a workman at the foundry round the corner. As if education and position and a gentlemanly employment were to count for nothing! Pure aristocratic insolence, that's just what I call it.'

Douglas Harrison looked across at him with a sort of pitying wonderment. 'I don't understand you,' he answered slowly. 'Do you mean to tell me, Maclaine, you don't think she's fit for you?'

'Don't think she's fit for me!' Maclaine

answered hotly. 'Do you want to insult me? Put it to yourself, my dear sir—I ask you, put it to yourself, and see how you'd like it! She's all very well to flirt with in a mild sort of way, but do you mean to say you'd *marry* Miss Figgins?'

Douglas Harrison rose and looked very solemnly into his friend's eyes. 'Marry her!' he echoed. 'Of course I'd marry her—if only she'd let me, and I could afford to keep her as she ought to be kept, like a cultivated lady. Marry her, Maclaine! Of course I'd marry her. Not fit for you, my dear fellow! Why, have you eyes in your head? She's fit for anything. She's fit to be a duchess.'

'Well, all I can say is,' Basil Maclaine retorted with a superior smile, 'I ain't a duke; but if I was, I could answer for one thing—I wouldn't agree with you.'

CHAPTER V.

AMONG THE BEST PEOPLE.

WHEN Saturday came—that much-hoped-for Saturday—Basil Maclaine rose all undismayed to the height of the occasion. He prepared himself elaborately for mingling in Good Society. No critical eye ever beheld a more gorgeous expanse of spotless white linen than Basil Maclaine's well-glazed shirt-front, a more faultless costume than Basil Maclaine's artistic suit of Scotch homespun dittos, a cleaner shave than Basil Maclaine's immaculate chin, a tighter fit than the pointed toes of Basil Maclaine's neat Oxford walking shoes. If Sabine Venables, that coveted heiress, had only known the desperate preparations Basil Maclaine indulged in beforehand for taking a pot-shot at her heart (and accompanying fortune), she would, at least, have felt flattered by the obvious importance which the handsome young civil servant evidently attached to the merest casual glance from those beady black eyes of hers. But, then, Sabine Venables was so thoroughly accustomed to being paid much court to by young men generally—for was she not the greatest catch in that corner of Surrey?—that one extra young man, more or less, to the tale of her conquests really made very little difference to her.

At Waterloo Station the two fellow-lodgers in Miss Figgins's furnished apartments for gentlemen met by appointment Douglas Harrison's journalistic brother, Hubert, the editor of that satirical print, the *Boomerang*.

'Charlie Simmons, of the War Office, is coming, too,' Maclaine ventured to observe as they took their seats in the train. 'Suppose we look out for him?'

'Oh no, don't let's,' Hubert Harrison

answered, making an ugly face. 'He's such awfully bad form. He's the sort of man, don't you know, who always sticks his invitation-cards in his looking-glass frame, by way of advertising his social importance.'

Basil Maclaine withdrew his head from the window at once, and made no answer. He had always looked upon Charlie Simmons himself as very 'good form' till that precise moment; but he registered a mental note now to avoid in future the social solecism—if such it were—which had brought a neatly-dressed and fair-spoken fellow-citizen under the ban of a censor who formed opinion in the public prints of his country. For Basil Maclaine was one of those numerous people who live entirely for the appearances of life, and have never, for even one solitary second, penetrated the fact that it has any solid realities at all behind them.

Charlie Simmons didn't happen to reach their apartment—in point of fact, he was travelling first; while Basil, who had taken a ticket for the same exalted mode of conveyance, had been hurried and bustled by his companions, unawares, into a third-class carriage—so they went down by themselves in that inferior vehicle all the way to Leatherhead. There, they walked up a long ridge, and past a handsome lodge, Hubert Harrison seeming to know the way particularly well, till, turning a corner in a leafy avenue, they came full in sight of a big house on a hilltop. It was a ruddy Queen Anne mansion of the very latest pattern, plumped down among immemorial elms and beeches.

'You've been here before, I see,' Basil Maclaine observed, as he stooped to brush the dust of the road off those neat Oxford walking shoes with his second-best handkerchief—the one he kept immured in his right coat-tail for such menial purposes, while the clean society rag resided habitually in his left breast-pocket.

'Dozens of times,' Hubert Harrison answered laconically.

'Then you know the people well?'

'Intimately,' the journalist responded, and lapsed into silence.

'It's a splendid place,' Basil Maclaine remarked, glancing round him in admiration. And indeed it was. He had never seen a nobler. The lawn of fine turf sloped gently down towards the Mickleham Valley, and being gracefully planted with well-ordered clumps of horse-chestnut, beech, and lime at irregular intervals, opened up delightful vistas down the wooded glen and across intervening ridges to the tower-topped height of Leith Hill in the distance. The sward in between lay smooth and close and velvety as a carpet. Great parterres of blossom diversified the foreground. Just at that moment, in the first full glory of summer foliage, the broad shady trees of Hurst Croft, against a fleecy blue and white sky, were a sight to rejoice the eye of any lover of nature. But it wasn't the picturesque beauty of the scene that struck Basil Maclaine with instant admiration and delight; it was the amplitude of the grounds, the spacious expanse of the lawn, the neatness of the roads and paths and flower-beds, the many outward and visible signs of extreme wealth and social importance. He saw in it, most of all, not a lovely stretch of hill country, but 'a magnificent place,' the external symbol of livery servants, horses, carriages, silver plate, diamonds, game preserves, dances, dinner-parties, and all the other vulgar gewgaws and festivities that his soul would have revelled in. He valued it at once as so much money's worth, and so much consideration in the eyes of society.

'Yes, there's a beautiful view,' Hubert Harrison answered, gazing vaguely away from the lawn and the foreground towards the varied outline of blue hills in the distance, rising one behind the other in long perspective. 'But Venables père is just a typical British Philistine of the first water. He doesn't deserve to live in such a lovely bit of wild country as this. He doesn't regard those trees of his as trees at all; he regards them as a magnificent lot of first-class timber.'

And poor Basil Maclaine had that moment been reflecting to himself that if only he had money to 'keep it up,' such a lovely bit of finely-timbered land as that would suit him down to the ground. For he, too, in his callow way, was an unfledged Philistine.

On the terrace in front of the windows half a dozen guests were already assembled, chatting in a group around Miss Venables and her father.

'Your friend Bertie Montgomery's here this afternoon, I see,' Douglas Harrison remarked, a little maliciously, to Basil, as they approached the group.

'Why do you call him Bertie?' the civil servant retorted, staring hard at all the guests in turn to see if he could possibly distinguish the scion of nobility from the common herd around him.

'I do it only in inverted commas,' Douglas Harrison answered, laughing.

'Which is he?' Basil asked at last, after a careful scrutiny. 'I thought you didn't know him. I . . . I was only pointed him out just once at Goodwood myself, and I don't remember him now very vividly.'

'The noisy young man in the noisy check suit,' Douglas Harrison replied, smiling. 'I hardly know him myself, though I meet him out sometimes; but Hubert and he have a nodding acquaintance. Come up, and let me introduce you to Miss Venables and her father.'

Basil hurried forward with his best company smile, and raised his hat politely with his first-class bow, as performed before ladies of the highest distinction only. He was a gentlemanly young man, in his way, as well as handsome; and if he could but for a moment have forgotten his profound respect for the externals of life, and considered somewhat its actualities, he might, perhaps, have turned out a very decent good fellow. As he raised his hat, responsive to Douglas's mention of her name, Sabine Venables made a gentle inclination of her head, and beamed softly upon him in her part as hostess. Basil Maclaine was vaguely aware of a tall, lithe figure, and a beautiful, graceful face, haughty and clear-cut, but intensely picturesque in its warm Southern beauty. She looked like the paintings he had seen—by Burgess, he fancied—of high-born Spanish ladies; the same proud curl of the lip, the same quick flash of the eyes, even the same faint suspicion of a dark, silky fringe around the delicate corners of that sensitive small mouth. Altogether, a young lady by no means to be trifled with, Miss Sabine Venables. Basil Maclaine, as he met her, came, saw, and was conquered.

A buzz of voices rang indefinitely on his ears. He murmured the usual commonplaces of first introduction about this lovely garden—such a charming day—the best month of the year to see England in—

delightful to get away from London dust and London mud to the clear blue skies and fresh air of the country. Then he fell back, inarticulate, into the second row, to catch and treasure up on the tablets of his soul what stray scraps might fall his way of the Best People's improving conversation.

'And where's your brother at present?' Charlie Simmons was asking in a familiar fashion of Lord Adalbert Montgomery. Charlie had followed them up close behind from the station, and greeted the descendant of antique Welsh princes with cordial affability, as indeed did also, to Basil's great surprise, both the Harrisons, for he had no idea they knew such very Good People.

'What, the Duke?' Lord Adalbert answered, stroking the ends of his almost imperceptible moustache with the attentive affection of early youth. 'Oh, he's all right; he's still at Homburg. Fluctuates pretty equally between there and Monte Carlo with great regularity, poor dear Powysland! Never by any chance goes near Llanfyllin Castle. A confirmed absentee, as Harrison says in the papers. Homburg in summer, Monte Carlo in winter, with flying visits to England just for the Oaks and Cesarewitch. Gambling himself to death at all of them, *as* usual.'

At this Lord Adalbert smiled sweetly, and Basil perceived that when he smiled he showed an even row of the whitest and pearliest teeth in all England. He was a good-looking young fellow enough, this Bertie Montgomery, and pleasant into the bargain, with that nameless incommunicable charm of manner which sometimes belongs as a hereditary gift to the youngest branches of our great old families.

'I should love to go to Monte Carlo so,' Sabine Venables put in; and as she spoke, all the young men, Lord Adalbert included, leant forward to listen; 'but papa won't take me. He's such a dreadful man about those things. He says it isn't proper.'

'My dear,' the typical British Philistine replied, with a deprecating cough, stroking his smooth-shaven chin, 'not at your present age, at least. The atmosphere's unsuited for you. In four or five years' time, perhaps; but not just at present.'

'In four or five years' time, perhaps,' Lord Adalbert said, smiling, 'Miss Venables may possibly have passed from your parental safe-keeping.'

'Very possibly,' Mr. Venables responded with a pleased and conscious air, rubbing his hands softly. 'Very possibly. Ve-ry possibly.'

'In that case,' Sabine said, looking around her like a queen upon her assembled court, and catching Hubert Harrison's eye as she spoke, 'I shall *make* whoever succeeds to the duty take me to Monte Carlo.'

'No doubt he'd be charmed,' Lord Adalbert answered, showing his teeth once more. 'I can imagine nothing more delightful than——'

'Mr. Maclaine,' Sabine put in, darting suddenly round upon him, and hauling him off in triumph to where she saw a lady of a certain age seated alone upon a garden bench, without anyone to talk to her, 'let me introduce you to Mrs. Bouverie-Barton—you've heard of Mrs. Bouverie-Barton, of course—ah! yes; I thought so.' Then, in a confidential undertone, 'You'll find her a most delightful and piquant talker, I'm sure. Very much spread about in society, you know. One of the most brilliant women in literary London.'

Thus withdrawn perforce from the circle round the throne and the inspiriting presence of Lord Adalbert Montgomery, Basil did his best to make himself agreeable, under depressing circumstances, to Mrs. Bouverie-Barton. Not that that clever lady, indeed, needed much entertaining. On the contrary, she included in herself, like a well-known journal, a perpetual fund of original entertainment. As Basil afterwards remarked to his friends, the Harrisons, the literary lady could talk like one o'clock.

'Yes, she's a beautiful girl, Sabine,' Mrs. Bouverie-Barton burst forth in answer to Basil's ingenuous outbreak of admiration for their charming young hostess. 'But it's a pity, for her own sake, she hasn't a mother to keep her in order. She's a desperate flirt—proud, but desperate. She coquettes eternally. And how absurdly she goes on with—oh dear no, I don't mean with *him*; she doesn't care twopence for poor Bertie, dear boy, though her father'd give his eyes for her to marry a Duke's brother—and a childless Duke, too, who's killing himself as hard as he can on the Continent. But I didn't mean with *him*. That's the merest flirtation—just love of power, the display of her fascination—but with a much more dangerous person—Hubert Harrison.'

'Hubert Harrison!' Basil exclaimed, looking up in surprise. 'You don't mean to say——'

But Mrs. Bouverie-Barton didn't even permit him to get a word in edgeways. 'Oh yes, I *do* mean to say,' she ran on, interrupting him; 'and it's true, every word of it. Just look at her now! Don't you see she's ostensibly talking to Lord Adalbert, and gazing at Lord Adalbert, and answering Lord Adalbert, but at every second word she says, for all that, she peeps out of the corners of her eyes, sideways, to see what Hubert Harrison thinks of what she's saying to him. I was a girl once myself—a long time ago—and I know the ways of them. She's leading Master Hubert a pretty dance, if anybody ever led him one. He's a clever boy, and a good-looking boy, and a nice boy; and if she doesn't ruin him, he has a great future before him still, for he's the smartest leader-writer in London this moment. But, take my word for it, she means to grind that boy to powder, like Lady Clara Vere de Vere, before she's done with him.'

'What! do you think she's in love with

him?' Basil Maclaine asked breathlessly. This odour of gossip about the Best People—and at first hand, too—was as incense in his nostrils.

'Love, my dear Mr. Maclaine—your name's Maclaine, isn't it? I thought that was how I caught it. Why, what century do you live in, and what on earth are you thinking of? You're talking archæology. Our young people nowadays know nothing of love—the fierce, unreasoning, inexplicable passion which moved the world when men and things were more natural. What they covet now is not hearts and darts, mutual flames, and so forth, but horses, jewellery, a title, an establishment. Young girls are taught the value of these things when they're the merest children, and they know the one way for them to earn them is by a good marriage. They're put in training for a match, and they know they're in training. Hair, figure, skin, voice, dancing, music, French accent, culture—all are of importance to them only as so many points to play in the marriage-market. The girl's brought out at last like a horse upon the course—as much uncovered as possible—and every step she takes, every triumph she makes, every costume, every conquest, every ball, every drawing-room, is blazoned abroad in all the vulgar publicity of the society papers. And when at last she catches her rich man, and nails him to her ear, they congratulate her publicly on having made very good running.'

Mrs. Bouverie-Barton paused, for want of breath, not want of words, and Basil Maclaine managed to interpose a hasty sentence. 'But Miss Venables has all these things already,' he said. 'She doesn't need them.'

By this time Mrs. Bouverie-Barton had recovered her breath, and began again excitedly. 'Of course not,' she flowed on in full flood. 'But young Harrison needs them, and he won't get them.. Poor young fellows, of course, never stand a chance of winning these great matrimonial lottery prizes. If the beauty's penniless, she's bought in by wealth; if the beauty's rich, she's bought in by title. Nothing for nothing's the rule of the bazaar. That's the first act; then comes the second. After marriage, these young people, hitherto only intent on selling themselves in the dearest market, suddenly discover, to their immense surprise, there's such a reality in the world as love—the love they despised—an irresistible energy—a force that sweeps down everything before it—money, position, honour, reputation. And what's the end of it all? The Divorce Court, disgrace, shame, misery, suicide!'

'What a Cassandra you are!' Basil Maclaine interposed with a visible effort to break the current. 'But you don't think, then, she'll marry Hubert Harrison?'

'Marry him?' Mrs. Bouverie-Barton cried with a scornful air. 'No. The idea's preposterous. Old Affability—they call the papa Old Affability, you know, for his smug manners—he'd never for a moment allow such a match, though she likes Hubert best. But she'll do as they all do. She'll marry Lord Adalbert first, and then, at the end of six months, she'll run away with Hubert. "My dear Bertie" will do for either, that's one comfort. She won't have the trouble of learning a new name when she runs away from her husband with the man she ought in the first instance to have married.'

'Then it's a usual case, you think?'

'Usual? Why, I've offered Lord Adalbert to bet him two to one in dozens of gloves that whoever he marries won't live a year with him. That was in confidence, of course; but he only smiled, and declined to take me. He's as jealous as a toad, you know; and he smiled, but he didn't at all like it.'

CHAPTER VI.

THE WAY OF THE WORLD.

Later in the afternoon, in another part of the grounds, Hubert Harrison met Sabine Venables face to face for a moment, behind a clump of low-feathering spruce firs, whose branches swept the ground, on the way to the refreshment-tent, in the far corner by the summer-house. Sabine smiled provokingly, and tried to trip on past him in her imperial, coquettish way. But the vigorous journalist was not so to be baulked. 'You mustn't go away so fast now, Sabine,' he said in a very low voice, planting himself right in front of her, and barring the path. 'I haven't had ten words yet the whole afternoon with you.'

'You've had more than ten looks, then,' the proud, handsome girl replied, with a little incipient curtsey. 'But what right have you got, I'd like to know, to say I mayn't go as fast and as far as I choose, sir?'

'No right,' the young man answered with mannish decision, 'except that I don't mean to let you, Sabine.'

'Oh my, how fine we are! How hoity-toity! Have I done anything, then, to offend your majesty?'

Hubert Harrison looked back at her, a half-jealous, half-admiring look. 'You've been talking all the time, without stopping, to that Bertie Montgomery man,' he answered, a little surlily.

'Well, and isn't it a hostess's duty to make herself agreeable to all her guests—even a Bertie Montgomery man?' Sabine replied, with just the suspicion of a toss of the head. 'Would you have me leave the entire remainder of my party uncared for, to wander about alone behind the trees with you, Mr. Harrison?'

'Mr. *What?*'

'Mr. Harrison.'

'Try again.'

'I won't.'

'Yes, you shall.'

'But I don't want to.'

'I don't care what you want. I'm a man, and must be obeyed.'

'Then with you, Hubert.'

She said it so prettily, with such a delicate inflexion of her lowered voice, and such a graceful modest droop of her long dark eye-lashes, that Hubert Harrison would have been more than human if he'd even pretended any longer to be seriously angry with her. Besides, being a man, and having bent her to his will, he was amply satisfied. 'That's right, Sabine,' he answered, standing a little way off and admiring her with his eyes. 'Now you're really nice. And how sweetly pretty you do look, to be sure, in that big Rembrandt-looking hat of yours!'

The proud girl relaxed once more, like any

village maiden. These proud girls always will to the one man who knows the exact right chord to touch upon. 'Do you think so?' she asked, glancing down at her dress with a quick eye of commendation. 'Do you think it suits me?'

'Suits you? Down to the ground,' the young man responded, measuring her with his gaze from head to foot. 'I never before saw you look so much as if you'd stepped straight out of a canvas of Velasquez.'

'Thank you,' the girl answered, with a little spot of colour rising unbidden to her cheek. 'I don't know why, Hubert, but whenever you pay me the least little bit of a compliment I think ten thousand times more of it than when——'

'Perhaps you like me a little bit better than any of them?' the young man suggested, interrupting her boldly.

'I never told you so, sir.'

'No, you never *told* me, I admit; but still, somehow——'

'Yes, beautifully blue, indeed, but not so fine as yesterday,' Sabine interposed of a sudden, with a warning look, as another couple passed by on the further side of the spruce firs. 'Now, my dear boy, how dreadfully imprudent and careless you are! You men have no gumption. Suppose that had been papa, or Mrs. Walker, my companion, and they'd overheard what you were talking about, what on earth would you have said to them?'

'I don't know, I'm sure, Sabine—except that I'm in love with you,' Hubert answered penitently, 'and I'm not ashamed of it. Now, don't go away yet, I'm not a quarter done. I haven't said half what I wanted to say to you.'

'I must,' Sabine interrupted. 'If I don't, it'll be noticed. Besides, you've said a great deal too much already.'

'Oh, nonsense, my dear child! You don't mean to tell me you've brought me all the way down from town to Leatherhead——'

'Oh well, if it's such a trouble to you to

come——' Sabine began, half pouting, and then broke off suddenly.

'But you're not going to put me off with just these few words. You'll give me an opportunity—Sabine—Sabine!'—he ran after her as she went—'there's something I want so much to say to you!'

'I know what it is,' the pretty coquette answered pettishly; 'and I'm not going to answer you. How can I, indeed, when you know dear papa has strictly ordered me—— And then there's Lord Adalbert! And your handsome friend with the black moustaches. He's so awfully good-looking. I'm neglecting my duty to all my guests, upon my word I am! I mustn't stop one minute more. I must really go—do let me. I must run back at once to them.'

'But, Sabine—one word! Miss Venables! Miss Venables!'

'Not one word more, Mr. Harrison. Take me back, will you, please, over yonder, by Mrs. Bouverie-Barton?'

For the rest of that afternoon, whether it was only to pique Hubert Harrison or not, Sabine Venables divided the greater share of her attention between Lord Adalbert Montgomery and Mr. Basil Maclaine of the Board of Trade. It's an ill wind that blows nobody good. Mr. Basil was delighted — in the seventh heaven. The Very Best People were taking him up. The heiress, indeed—most important of all—was making herself specially agreeable to him. She walked about with him through the grounds as she had refused to do with Hubert Harrison; and showed him the conservatories; and Basil took the privilege as a high compliment. Alas! how little he knew the by-ways and anfractuosities of the female heart! Had he been better skilled in the intricate windings of that interminable maze, he might have been well aware that with a girl of Sabine Venables' type the distinction by no means implied a special preference. Your true proud coquette gives little encouragement to the man she really likes: she's affable and natural only to those men whom she regards in her own soul as hopelessly and entirely outside the running.

But as Basil Maclaine's philosophy didn't embrace that psychologic principle, he hugged himself all the afternoon on the flattering discovery that Miss Venables was in fact very much taken with him.

And indeed, he said to himself, if a sharp-eyed woman of the world, like Mrs. Bouverie-Barton, thought Sabine Venables displayed a distinct preference for a penniless journalist like Hubert Harrison, why on earth should it be so absurd to think she might also display a similar preference—which, of course, could conceivably ripen with time into a more commercially valuable feeling—for himself, Basil Maclaine of the Board of Trade, every bit as good a fellow any day as Hubert, and a long sight handsomer into the bargain? Why should one take it for granted that these great tufts, like Bertie Montgomery, had all the hearts of the game in their aristocratic hands as well as all the diamonds? For his own part, Basil Maclaine detested and despised these petty class distinctions—when they told against him. He didn't see why a girl like Sabine Venables—even if she did happen to be rich and to be brought up in a big house and in good society (among the Best People), and all that kind of thing—need necessarily prefer a courtesy lord, with no brains to brag about and an incipient moustache, to a clever and sensible and well-educated young man, say, for example, in one of her Majesty's Government offices. For whenever it came to the classes above him, Basil Maclaine was a leveller of the deepest dye; though when he had to deal, per contra, with the classes below, he never could understand how anybody on earth could possibly be so rude and so wanting in discrimination as to confound him for one moment with such a scrubby lot of cads and greengrocers.

This is a common trait in the highly stratified English mind. It ignores the existence of strata above, except when it wants to get into them, but it recognises the existence of strata below as vastly beneath it.

Once, indeed, in the course of the afternoon, Basil came up a second time with Mrs. Bouverie-Barton, who was imparting her views on the present crisis in the marriage market to his fellow-lodger, Douglas Harrison, much as she had imparted them, in a full-flowing river of speech, to his own attentive ears somewhat earlier in the day's entertainment. 'For my part,' she was saying, as Basil joined their colloquy, 'I've always maintained it was an error for any person, either man or woman, to marry for money. Why, the Bible even tells us how Rebekah, daughter of Laban—or was it his sister? I really forget which; these things go from one so unless one teaches in a Sunday-school—was tempted by jewels of gold and fine raiment to marry a man she'd never seen and couldn't possibly love; and what was the consequence? She became a tricky, deceitful, rapacious wife, and brought misery into his house unto the third and fourth generation. What I say is, a man and a woman ought to marry to please themselves. They ought to take the person who will make them happy.'

'Yes,' Basil interposed briskly, turning the conversation in the direction of his own thoughts. 'How absurd that a woman should be taught to look down upon a man who is really and truly her equal in everything, just on the ground of some foolish difference in the accidentals of position.'

'Quite so,' Douglas Harrison answered, veering towards him sharply with a look full of suggestion. 'And how absurd that a man should venture to look down upon a woman immeasurably his superior in every valuable quality, just because he thinks her relations have something or other to do with some decent trade or some honest handicraft which he considers beneath him.'

Basil Maclaine winced, and said no more for the moment. He hardly recovered his equanimity, indeed, till Mrs. Bouverie-Barton turned to him, on the eve of her departure, and said in her blandest society tone, "I'm at home every Wednesday during the season at ten, Mr. Maclaine, if you care to drop in at my little gathering some evening. Wednesday, at ten: don't forget! But there!—I'll send you a card in the course of a day or two."

Then Basil's spirits rose high in that internal barometric tube of his with a sudden rebound of anti-cyclonic energy. He felt he was indeed making progress by rapid strides among the Best People.

They went home by train together, Charlie Simmons and all; and, by extreme good luck, just as they were on the point of leaving the station, who should espy them but Lord Adalbert Montgomery, who, with astounding condescension, to Basil's immense surprise, jumped into their third-class carriage without a moment's hesitation, and rode all the way up to town with them in a very good humour. "That's the way with your great swells," Basil thought to himself admiringly. "They're too sure of their position to be afraid of belittling themselves." He talked to Basil more than to any of the rest; perhaps because Basil took most pains to cultivate him; and when they shook one another's hands warmly at parting, he said, with most marked friendliness, "Good-bye, Machiavel. Drop in and see me some night at the Die and Hazard when you're passing." Basil hadn't the slightest idea in the world what particular club he meant to indicate by that affectionate nickname, and he didn't like to display his ignorance of the subject before both the Harrisons by asking him; but he thought to himself, as he walked home with his two friends, that, after all, these Really Big People aren't such bad sort of fellows when you come to know them; and he reflected with pride that he had now earned the right to speak before all and sundry of 'Bertie Montgomery' without the liability to be stumped any more by that awkward and disconcerting little question, 'Do you know him?' 'Know him? Of course I do!' he could retort glibly in future, with the joyous exuberance of his kind. 'Met him down at my friends, the Venables', at Hurst Croft, near Leatherhead, at a garden-party; and he asked me to look in upon him some evening at the Die and Hazard.'

Only once in the course of their homeward walk (for Hubert was to dine with them) did either of the Harrisons allude in any way to their distinguished acquaintance, and even then they didn't overtly mention him by name. It was at the end of a long and deep pause, during which each man pursued his own train of thought uninterruptedly. Then Douglas broke the silence with an abrupt sentence, whose personal pronouns bore no obvious relation to any known antecedent. 'I don't believe she'd take him,' he said. 'even if he asked her.'

'Don't know, I'm sure,' Hubert answered gloomily. 'She's such an enigma. Her father'd do his best, of course, to make her accept him.'

'I don't think he asked her to-day,' Douglas went on reflectively.

'I don't think he did. He can't quite make up his mind to take the plunge. That's the worst of these fellows. They feel so beastly sure they can throw their handkerchief at whoever they like, that they keep watching and waiting till they're certain they've got the pick of all possible chances. Confound their impudence!'

'She doesn't care a pin for him,' Douglas went on decisively.

'Oh no, she doesn't *care* a pin for him, *of course!* but she's so very uncertain. There are such a lot of sides to the question to be considered. I'm never quite sure she won't do in the end exactly as her father tells her.'

That same evening, at Hurst Croft, when

dinner was finished and the servants had withdrawn, and Mrs. Walker had retired to her own room, the typical British Philistine, sitting bolt upright at the head of his table, with his clean-shaven face and mutton-chop whiskers, looking the pink of respectability, raised his eyes suddenly and met his daughter's. 'Well, Sabine?' he murmured with an inquiring gaze.

'Well, papa?'

'Did anything happen?'

'Why, lots of things happened, of course, didn't they?'

'Oh yes; but did he ask you?'

'Did who ask me?'

'Lord Adalbert.'

'Ask me what?'

The typical British Philistine stroked his chin softly. 'Ask you anything, Sabine,' he said in an evasive way. He had too much respect for the conventionalities of his Philistine creed to commit himself right out even before his own daughter.

'No, papa; he asked me nothing'—this almost snappishly.

'He was very attentive,' her father interposed.

'They're all attentive, always,' Sabine muttered, unconcerned.

The typical British Philistine stroked his chin once more. 'If he were to ask you anything——' he began in an inquiring voice.

But Sabine cut him short at once with an angry flash of those fierce Southern eyes of hers. 'If he were to ask me anything, how on earth can I tell you,' she said, 'what answer I'd give him until I've heard his question? How on earth do I know what he's likely to ask? Why on earth should I bother about him? The young man doesn't interest me. That's all I know about it.'

The typical British Philistine stroked his chin, somewhat dismayed at her vehemence, for the third time. 'It's very annoying,' he said once more in an aggrieved tone, 'that this matter doesn't come to a head one way or the other. I've reasons of my own—very important reasons—for wishing to get the matter settled offhand before I go on to . . . eh . . . to other business arrangements.'

CHAPTER VII.

SHARP PRACTICE.

'I've never been inside a court before,' Linda said to her brother on the morning appointed for Mr. Arthur Roper's trial; 'but I really think I must spare time to go, just for once, to-day. Mr. Harrison tells me he can pass me in; and I want to see what any other barrister can possibly find to say in the burglar's defence—it seems so hopeless.'

Cecil Figgins looked up from the wheels and cranks of his model at the table by the window, and wiped his greasy hands on the duster at his side as he answered slowly, 'Well, do as you like, Linda. In fact, now I come to think of it, you usually *do* do as you like, whether I ask you to or not. But mind you don't forget to call on the way for that cyanide of potassium. I can't do without it much longer. I'm getting the thing splendidly into working order this morning. It almost runs now. Another sleepless night or two'll set the wheels going all round like wildfire.'

'I wish you didn't depend quite so much on sleepless nights, Cecil,' Linda put in with a faint sigh. 'I know it's the time your best ideas always come to you, but I think, in the end, you must certainly pay for it. Mr. Harrison says the physiological cost's too great in the long-run. You've got to make up for it, sooner or later, one way or the other.'

'Bother the physiological cost!' Cecil responded frankly. 'The machine's the thing; and the machine's progressing like a high-pressure steam-engine. It's the high-pressure that does it; and it's a hundred times better than a steam-engine, too. It's the motor of the future, I can tell you that.

There's nothing like it. It's going to lick creation.'

So in due time Linda set off alone for the Central Criminal Court, as the newspapers call it, at the door of which Douglas Harrison, in wig and gown, was waiting to receive her and pass her in to a place reserved for her. She looked so neat and trim in her plain jacket and hat — all home-made, but all fitting like tailor work — that Douglas wondered how even Basil Maclaine, with his conventional measures, could fail to take her for the lady she really was. But it was no time just then for him to indulge in sentimentalities; for Mr. Arthur Roper's case was on, as he himself phrased it, and Mr. Arthur Roper, *in propriâ personâ*, resplendent in new clothes, a perfect triumph of the sartorial art, stood smiling in the dock with easy assurance, and quizzed the witness through his single eye-glass like one who took but a distant interest in the legal proceedings.

It was wonderful how different Mr. Roper

appeared, now that he stood there on his best behaviour, with innocence on his front and a rose in his buttonhole, from the cynical criminal who had disgusted Douglas Harrison in that bare cell at Holloway Gaol by his undisguised wickedness. He was, to all outward appearance, a most unblemished gentleman of scholastic taste, neatly arrayed in a black morning suit, and with linen as spotless as Basil Maclaine's own; for Mr. Roper was a person who thoroughly understood the value of the contrast between his own external appearance (at its best) and the nature of the profession he so gaily exercised. He looked that moment the exact embodiment of British respectability. He was posing, in fact, as the victim of misapprehension. Douglas Harrison saw at a glance that the defence to be set up would evidently be one of mistaken identity. So much, indeed, the brief he received had already informed him.

But how was a plea of mistaken identity

possible after Mr. Roper's own frank—not to say brutal—admissions as to the details of his costume at the moment of his capture? A man who walks about the streets of London with the instrument playfully described as 'a sectional jemmy' concealed upon his person, and who is taken red-handed in hiding in an attic in somebody else's house, at an advanced hour of the evening, must surely be *ipso facto* proclaimed a burglar! Douglas Harrison waited with professional interest to see what some less puritanical counsel than himself could manage to do in the way of gratifying Mr. Roper's aspirations after continued freedom.

A brilliant young barrister, Erskine by name, and Scotch by ancestry, with an inquiring face, thick sensuous lips, and a wig pushed back somewhat from his freckled forehead, had stepped into the brief Douglas Harrison had vacated. Linda, gazing hard at his shifty gray eyes and dubious mouth, came at once to the conclusion that the brilliant young barrister, for all his jauntiness, was well equipped for the battle of life by possession of the invaluable quality of unscrupulousness. While the police witnesses and the servants at the house were giving their evidence in chief, the brilliant young barrister, leaning back in his seat with his hands in his pockets and his lips pursed up into a critical sneer, regarded them keenly, yet with a well-assumed air of complete indifference. But as soon as it came to his turn to cross-examine, he rose in his place exulting, and pounced down upon them at once, like a hawk upon its quarry. Those helpless, floundering, blundering policemen, with their hazy ideas and their easy identifications, were as rats in the terrier's mouth to the acute and well-trained intelligence of the brilliant young barrister. He muddled their thick brains by his subtle distinctions; he shook them till they were too terrified to answer yes or no; he reduced them at once by his ingenious questions and ingenuous suggestions to a complete pulp of general vague scepticism as to everybody's individuality and everybody's identity.

'Did they arrest his client then and there in the attic?'

'No, not just at first; he gave them a run for it.'

'Oh! *he* gave them a run for it, did he? Who? the man in the attic?'

'Yes, the prisoner.'

The brilliant young barrister, throwing back his head and adjusting his *pince-nez* with an infinite air of forensic cunning, would be obliged if they would carefully answer his question—yes or no. '*Which* gave them a run for it—the man in the attic, or that gentleman in the dock there?'

Witnesses, one after another, each scratching his head, or fumbling with his buttons, and regarding the prisoner askance with very doubtful eyes, repeated vaguely, 'The man in the attic.'

Then the brilliant young barrister followed

them up briskly. 'He gave them a run for it, did he, this man in the attic? Well, which way did he run? Was he in sight all the time? How far did they follow him?'

'Oh, they followed him, as it might be, a little way round the corner, and there they caught him at last, running up against a lady.'

'Ah, yes, exactly so; we knew all that. But did they ever lose sight of him?'

Witnesses faltered and prevaricated feebly. Some of them did, some of them didn't. Then the brilliant young barrister, leaning forward inquisitively, like a weasel on the trail, pursued them once more with doubts and suggestions. 'They saw a man running away; yes, that was clear; but what man exactly? There were several people in the street at the time, weren't there?'

'Well, a good few, certainly.'

'Oh, a good few! He thought so. And the man in the attic lost his hat as he ran out into the street, didn't he?'

'Yes, he lost his hat.'

'And round the corner they caught a man, his client, this gentleman in the dock here, who was also hatless?'

'Yes, that was so.'

'And the reason they identified the man in the attic with that gentleman in the dock there, at a moment's sight, on a dark night, under the glare of the lamps, in a street with a good few people in it, was simply and solely because he'd lost his hat, wasn't it?'

Witnesses faltered, and could hardly be certain. They *thought* he was the same man. He looked like him, and was dressed like him then. But now he was dressed differently.

'Oh, he looked like him, and was dressed like him! Well, now we are getting to it. But the man in the attic was wearing a hat with the lining turned down so as to form a mask, the hat that Constable B 38 had produced—yes, I see it, thank you—so that witnesses never saw his face at all. They must have judged, therefore, entirely by his clothes and his figure. Now, would they please be very careful; they were on their oaths, remember. What sort of clothes was the man in the attic wearing when they saw him?'

And there, of course, the brilliant young barrister got all the usual contradictions and cross-statements with which frequenters of courts are only too familiar, half the witnesses being a great deal too vague, and the other half a great deal too definite.

At last the brilliant young barrister played his trump card, as far as cross-examination went. 'Would the police kindly hand him that hat—the hat they picked up in the road immediately after the arrest—the hat with the lining cut into a mask—the hat that had undoubtedly belonged to the man in the attic?'

The constable, with some reluctance and many misgivings, handed over the crucial incriminating object.

Then counsel turned, very apologetically,

to the gentleman in the dock there. 'Will you excuse me, sir,' he said, in his politest and blandest voice, as one who ventures upon asking a very great favour. 'I know it must be most unpleasant to you to have to try on another man's hat—and that man a common burglar, too—but under the circumstances, you know, to further the ends of justice. . . . Oh, thank you, so much, thank you. Of course, it may just happen to fit you, or, again, it may not; it's a mere idea of mine—but, still, as a matter of experiment—no, not that way please; turn *down* the lining; the burglar was wearing it over his face as a mask, you know, and that's what I want to see, whether it would fit you or not that way.'

Mr. Roper took the hat gingerly, between finger and thumb, and, holding it so at arm's length for a moment, examined it with an air of profound disgust. Then, like a man who makes up his mind to perform a disagreeable duty in the cause of truth and justice, at no matter what cost to his personal feelings, he placed it on his head, with an evident effort, and let it fall down naturally, as it would, about him.

There was a sensation in court.

It simply extinguished him!

The burglar's hat was three sizes too large for the gentleman in the dock; and the brilliant young barrister turned round, demonstrative, with a silent but triumphant smile to the jury.

When it came to the defence, Mr. Erskine and his client had things all their own way. 'So remarkable a case of police blundering,' the brilliant young barrister said, 'had seldom or never come under his notice. The constables meant well, no doubt, but they were clumsy and incompetent. His client, a respectable gentleman of education and some small means, in the musical profession, in fact, and recently engaged at a well-known theatre, had been out that evening, as the evidence would show, walking with a lady of his acquaintance; a lady, to be quite definite (he was sorry to be obliged to refer to matters which ought to be private, but he had no choice in the case), to whom he had for some time being paying marked attentions, with a view to matrimony. He believed he was right in saying his client and the young lady were engaged to one another. The hour was late, it was true; but the lady, whom he would produce, was employed as a nursery-governess during the day, and could only meet her *fiancé* accordingly at an advanced period of the evening. Mr. Roper, his witnesses would prove to them, had just parted from the lady at the corner of the street, when he heard a loud shouting and a noise in front as of a sudden riot. Fearing that the Socialists or the Red Indians at Olympia had broken loose, or that the Salvation Army was performing midnight drill, or that some other danger to life and limb menaced society in general and the lady in particular, he turned back at once to protect her, as any one of *you* would have done under similar circumstances, gentlemen, and ran hastily in that direction; when, to his surprise, he found himself pursued and hustled by a howling mob of policemen, servants, bystanders, and loafers, including, no doubt, the actual burglar himself, who was perhaps, indeed, the very man that knocked off his client's hat, as he passed, into the mud of the roadway. Alarmed and astonished, his client ran a little way, hatless, till he came up with the lady, when, to his profound astonishment, he found himself bullied, seized, and arrested before her very eyes on a charge of burglary—a crime of which the jury had only to look at the educated gentleman in the dock for a moment to see that he was, and must be, wholly and entirely incapable. He would call first'—here a deep hush—'Miss Elizabeth Pomeroy.'

There was a stir in court as Miss Elizabeth Pomeroy, a delicate and modest-looking girl, in a plain dark dress, and a very quiet, almost Quakerish, bonnet, stepped into the witness-box. Miss Elizabeth Pomeroy was slight but pretty; her hair was plaited at the back in a neat coil that alone betokened the utmost respectability, and her accent was that of an educated lady. She gave her evidence with a graceful, shrinking timidity, which produced at once an immediate effect upon the susceptible hearts of the gentlemen of the jury. The story she told was short and simple. She had just left her friend, Mr. Roper, at the street corner when the tumult (as she called it) occurred, and she saw him a minute afterwards returning towards her, breathless, in great agitation. Another man, running past him at full speed, bare-headed himself, knocked off Mr. Roper's hat into the road, and then disappeared, like lightning, round another corner. The next thing she knew, the police were upon them like a herd of wild beasts, and they shook Mr. Roper, and behaved most shamefully to him, 'though

I explained it all to them,' the witness said simply; 'but they *wouldn't* listen to me, and they *would* arrest him.' Here was Mr. Roper's hat which she picked up afterwards from the gutter, all muddy as she found it. But the police had insisted upon giving him another hat which they picked up round the corner, thrown away, with a queer-looking instrument they called a jemmy and the bull's-eye lamp that had been produced already by the police witnesses.

Cross-examination didn't do much to shake Miss Pomeroy's credit; and, indeed, the jury took it rather ill that so pretty and modest a young girl should be so roughly handled by the counsel for the prosecution. The other witnesses were of the familiar sort who didn't see anything themselves to speak of, and who were of opinion that nobody else saw anything either.

The judge, a sceptical-looking gentleman with sandy whiskers, summed up, as was his wont, with luminous indecision. This was a case of disputed identity. The police took the prisoner in the dock for a well-known expert thief, and believed he was the man they found in the attic when the alarm was raised by the servants of the family. If the jury agreed with them, then, and in that case, they must find him guilty. The prisoner's counsel had offered them an alternative explanation—a most ingenious explanation—and had brought up a witness—he must say a very straightforward witness—to prove his theory. If they believed that witness, whose evidence was partially corroborated by the facts about the hat, they must acquit the prisoner as the victim of an unfortunate error of judgment. If, on the contrary, they disbelieved the witness, but failed to see that the prosecution had proved the identity of the man in the attic with the prisoner before them, then they must give the prisoner the benefit of the doubt. And the jury, thus admonished, after a very short retirement, returned to court to announce that, on serious consideration, they couldn't feel sure the police were not mistaken.

'Then you find a verdict of not guilty?' the judge said sharply.

'Yes, my lord,' the foreman answered.

'The prisoner is discharged,' the judge observed loudly, with a cynical smile. Then, in a theatrical aside: 'And he may thank his lucky stars for having got off so easily.'

Mr. Arthur Roper smiled in return, bowed politely to the judge with the sandy whiskers, stroked his moustache, and sauntered from the dock with easy nonchalance. The brilliant young barrister, by fair means or foul, had turned him loose once more, a free man, for another campaign against the society of his fellows.

At the bar he turned, and gazed blandly at the judge. 'I beg your pardon, my lord,' he said with charming effrontery, 'but—may I have my hat?' and he pointed towards the one he had tried on just before with such well-assumed disgust.

The court laughed aloud, and the judge, with a smile, said: 'Policeman, give it up to him.'

As Linda and Douglas Harrison walked home together, both intent on their own thoughts, the girl broke the silence at last by saying abruptly, 'I'm more glad than ever now you didn't accept that brief, Mr. Harrison.'

'So'm I, Linda,' Douglas answered. 'While I listened to that fellow's cross-examination it made me ashamed of my profession. The man's a rogue to act so. He knew it was all lies. He knew that woman Pomeroy was just going through a clever piece of amateur acting. When I think how much harm a fellow like him may do the world by throwing dust in the eyes of an ignorant jury, I almost regret I was ever called to the bar.'

'And yet,' Linda said thoughtfully, 'there's another side to it, too. How much good a man may do in helping to save some innocent person against all appearances to the contrary!

Some day, perhaps, you'll get such a chance; and if ever you do, you'll be glad you're a barrister.'

'Perhaps I shall,' Douglas answered carelessly. He thought little of the words then; but years after he remembered them on due occasion with a thrill of pleasure.

Meanwhile, at a bar near the court they had just quitted, Mr. Arthur Roper, his own master once more, was celebrating his release from temporary detention over a bottle of champagne with Miss Elizabeth Pomeroy.

'Well, that was a near shave this time, Bess!' the head of the profession said, holding his glass to hers and clinking it merrily. 'You're a brick, and no mistake! If it hadn't been for you, my dear, blow me if I wouldn't have been in Queer Street by this time.'

'But he's a clever young chap, too, that lawyer fellow,' Miss Pomeroy answered, raising the glass to her lips and meeting his eyes with hers. 'He pulled it through splendid. We must give him a lift with the trade. Here's his very good health. Mr. Erskine! Mr. Erskine! The other one was a muff; he'd never have done the job. But what licks me quite, Arthur, is why on earth your own hat that you dropped in the street didn't fit you.'

Mr. Roper exploded in a short paroxysm of internal merriment. Then he lowered his voice confidentially. 'My own idea!' he murmured. 'A capital invention. Steel spring inside the cork that lines the billycock. It keeps the cork pressed out while you wear it tight against the head. When I threw away the hat, I jerked out the spring, and nobody noticed it. First-rate dodge for once. But if one tried it twice, the police'd find out. Altogether, I never did a better or narrower escape in all my life; for if you hadn't been waiting about outside in your neat get-up to help me with the swag it'd have been all up with me. Here's my love to you, Bess, with your neat back hair; and may you live long, and keep out of the stone jug for ever!'

CHAPTER VIII.

DRAMATIC INTELLIGENCE.

A FEW days later Basil Maclaine was thrown into a perfect fever of excitement by receiving a note, very cordially worded, from Sabine Venables. This was more than he had hoped almost! He was getting into the very thick of Good Society now, and no mistake. He was beginning to be recognised. Last Wednesday he had been introduced to no end of the Best People at Mrs. Bouverie-Barton's 'little gathering' of two hundred souls; and to-day, here was what the heiress of Hurst Croft herself wrote to him—and on a tiny pink sheet of notepaper, too, with her crest and monogram in gold and colours:

'Dear Mr. Maclaine,

'I've only just learned from Mr. Hubert Harrison, who is good enough to assist me in my little project, that you're quite a great swell at amateur theatricals; and as we are going to get up a Pastoral Play in the grounds at Hurst Croft, I venture to ask you whether we might count upon your kind aid in arranging the piece, and, if possible, also in taking a part for us. The performance will take place about July 20, and the play we have chosen is "As You Like It." As far as yet arranged, the cast will include Lord Adalbert Montgomery as Orlando, Mr. Harrison as Jaques, Miss Weatherley as Celia, and myself as Rosalind. We wonder whether it would suit you to undertake the part of Touchstone — which Mr. Harrison says you would render admirably. If you could do us the favour of answering at an early date, you would greatly oblige

'Yours very sincerely,

'Sabine Estelle Venables.'

Basil Maclaine leant back in his chair as he read that note in a delicious ecstasy of self-congratulation. To be sure, there were drawbacks and difficulties in the way; he didn't for one moment disguise them from himself.

Bertie Montgomery was to have the part of Orlando—the part that allowed him to play most tenderly upon the Rosalind's feelings; the part that anybody with a spark of regard for the heiress's heart (and Basil Maclaine had fallen really in love with her, in his own way) would most have chosen for himself, and most have regretted to see falling to the share of his more fortunate rival. But there was no help for that. No doubt Old Affability, the typical British Philistine, her papa (who seemed to Basil Maclaine a perfect model of all that an elderly English gentleman of the banking persuasion ought to be), had settled that if 'As You Like It' was to come off at all in his grounds, nobody but Lord Adalbert should play Orlando to his daughter's

Rosalind. And quite right, too—from the papa's point of view, Basil thought to himself frankly; for he was candid enough to admit, after all, that if *he* were a papa, and banking were his profession, he would like his daughters to marry among the very Highest and Noblest in the land—the Best and Greatest. It must be such a consolation to one's declining years, you know, to feel one's self the father-in-law of a Duke's brother!

But then Touchstone! He could have wished, indeed, it had been any other part in the play but Touchstone. To be sure, the make-up was most becoming to him, with his dark complexion and black moustache; but the part itself was certainly not a dignified one. He hated comedy—though he succeeded best in it. Hubert Harrison was to be the Jaques. He'd have liked Jaques well enough; there was sentiment in that, and philosophy, too; and melancholy is so gentlemanly! But the Fool of the play! It was really most unkind of her to put him off, black moustache and all, with making love in by-play to that ridiculous Audrey!

Still, it's something to be asked to take part in a Pastoral Play at all—pastoral plays were just then very fashionable—and it's something to have your name mixed up with a lord's and to be reported in *Truth*, and to feel that if you're only playing the fool, you're playing it, at least, in the very Best Society. Basil Maclaine was by no means unsusceptible to these varied charms; and when he wrote back, as he meant to do, 'I shall be only too delighted,' the phrase would contain a degree of truth that is very unusual with it.

Linda came in to clear away breakfast as he was still gazing with admiration at the crest and monogram. In the simplicity of his heart (for, like most of his kind, Basil was, after all, a simple-hearted young man, who expected the whole world to feel about everything exactly as he did), he handed her the letter. Linda read it through with careful scrutiny. 'You won't be able to get away from the office for the rehearsals, will you?' was her first practical comment.

Basil, who had expected hushed awe and congratulation at so magnificent a programme, gazed back at her, almost speechless. 'Oh yes,' he answered, after a pause. 'For an affair like *this*, I can manage to make arrangements. It's the sort of thing one doesn't get asked to every day, Linda.'

'They might have invited you to take a better part than Touchstone,' the girl went on, her pride for her lover a little piqued by the selection. 'But I suppose it's all right. Whatever part you're cast for you always act so admirably.'

'And then, look at the company!' Basil answered with pride. 'Lord Adalbert Montgomery!'

'So I see,' Linda said, without a tinge of admiration in her voice, exactly as if the man were a mere Tom, Dick, or Harry. 'And Miss Venables is to be Rosalind. I . . . I'm glad you're not her Orlando. It's such a ridiculous position for a man to have to assume—all that sighing and love-song making about a woman you don't really care a pin for.'

Basil Maclaine stared hard at her with a sudden twinge of his accusing conscience. Could the girl actually think he was in love with *her* in the sort of way that would interfere with his making love in real earnest to Sabine Venables? He took Linda's hand, unresisted this time, in his. 'She's a very pretty girl, Linda,' he said, gently pressing it.

'So I hear,' Linda answered, looking him back in the face fearlessly; for it never even occurred to her honest heart what Basil was driving at.

'And very rich,' Basil went on, imagining he was disillusioning her.

'Very rich,' Linda replied, with a certain proud intonation in her clear, deep voice. 'And the sort of girl any man might be glad to sell himself for.'

She looked beautiful as she said it, in that

native pride of her womanhood that was perfectly natural to her. It was a shot fired at random, but it took effect. Basil was holding her hand in his own. All men are human —especially, I have observed, when a beautiful woman's hand is clasped tight in theirs. Basil faltered, and was lost. 'But not half so pretty or half so good as you, Linda,' he murmured, much lower.

'Thank you,' Linda answered, and pressed his hand back. Then she felt this had gone quite far enough for the present; and in her matter-of-fact way she lifted the tray, and glided from the room. Basil glanced after her with an approving look. 'Viewed merely as a woman,' he said to himself frankly, with unwonted candour, 'upon my word, she's worth a round dozen of the other one! If she were only in one's own position in life, now. But there! one mustn't be a fool. Hang it all! one must marry a woman, at least, whose relations one wouldn't be ashamed of before one's own children.'

And the things of which Basil Maclaine would have been ashamed were not petty meannesses or vulgarities of ingrained nature, but the crime of poverty or the misdemeanour of living outside Society. *Noblesse oblige*; and he felt that much was now demanded of a Government servant who had begun to mix with the Best People.

For the next week or two, however, in the intervals which the daily service of his country allowed him, Basil Maclaine was perpetually down at Hurst Croft, arranging and rehearsing for 'As You Like It.' The evenings were long just then; and by taking the first train after office hours he was able to get three hours of daylight in the country still, and to rehearse to his heart's content with the rest of the company.

These meetings on the lawn at Hurst Croft did him two good turns. In the first place, they allowed him to see a great deal of Sabine Venables, who was courtesy itself to him. And, in the second place, they enabled him, by dexterous railway arrangements, to improve his acquaintance with Bertie Montgomery. He was quite in the swim of things now, he said to himself each day gaily.

But as there is a thorn to every rose, it must be added in justice that Basil would have enjoyed the rehearsals a vast deal more if it had not been for the constant presence of Hubert Harrison, who discussed minor points of detail in private far more often than was necessary with Sabine Venables, and of his brother Douglas, who cast a glance of disapproval upon Basil himself whenever he ventured to bask too freely in the sunshine of the heiress's fickle favour. Nor did he care for the frequent paternal supervision of Old Affability himself, whose bland City smile—too much like a superior banking version of the draper's assistant's for Basil's own austere fancy—asserted itself for ever in the foreground, with all the pertinacity of a Cheshire cat, when Sabine ventured for a moment to talk to anybody on earth except the favoured scion of a ducal house. Indeed, in more than one particular, Basil found Old Affability very much in the way. Especially as regarded that pale little creature who was cast for Celia, and in whom the master of Hurst Croft appeared to feel a fatherly interest out of all proportion, Basil thought, to her face or fortune.

This feeble little girl was named Woodbine Weatherley; she had been at school with Sabine, and, being 'intellectual,' as they call it, had afterwards gone to Girton, where her mind, such as it was, had wholly got the better of her frail small body. She was Woodbine by name, and Woodbine by nature. She seemed specially intended by Providence to cling for support to somebody or something; but, unhappily, so far as Basil could perceive, Providence had unkindly neglected to provide her with anybody or anything in particular to cling to. Mr. Venables insisted she should take the part of Celia; and she was well cast for it—if she was to be cast at all—for there was no other character in the whole play she could possibly have been entrusted with. Basil accepted her aid politely, though with a very bad grace, and did his best to mould her by continued training into a passable Celia. She would have preferred a Greek play herself, she said; she thought she could act Antigone; but, failing that, she really did her level best for Shakespeare.

All through the rehearsals, however, no matter what else went right or wrong, Old Affability, regardless for the moment of the thrilling fact that Consols had closed at ninety-four and seven-eighths for the account, appeared to concern himself about two things alone—whether Lord Adalbert and Sabine were conferring together enough over their respective parts, and whether Woodbine Weatherley was having full justice done to her talent by stage-manager and fellow-actors or actresses.

'Papa's so kind to her,' Sabine said, when Basil made some laughing remark to the heiress one day about his obvious solicitude that Miss Weatherley should receive her due share of applause. 'He's very good, you know, in his way, to poor people, papa is. He likes to befriend them. Woodbine's an orphan, I suppose you've heard, and she wants to be a high school teacher, or something of the sort—all the girls nowadays are mad to be high school teachers or else hospital nurses; it's the craze of the moment. They call it a mission. But papa thinks she's not quite strong enough for missions, and he'd like to find her some easier work. Poor little thing, she has a hard life of it, I'm afraid! There's not enough of her for any man ever to fall in love with, of course; so she's not likely to marry: and she isn't strong enough to earn her own living, I think; so I dare say in the end we shall have to keep her. She won't cost much to keep, that's one good thing. It's positively dreadful to see her at dinner. She takes a tiny little slice off a chicken's breast, and then leaves the best part of it, and never digests the remainder. She's a sort of chameleon, I believe, or is it a salamander? She lives off air, flavoured with notes on the Greek tragedians.'

'Is she so learned, then?' Basil asked, with a superior smile.

'Learned!' Sabine rejoined. 'Why, I should rather think so. She's nothing else. She's got the classics on the brain, and all she thinks about on earth is Æschylus and the practice of the Christian virtues. As if *those* were the kind of things men ever care for!'

An heiress is always much franker in admissions of this sort than any other unmarried woman. She's so accustomed to being openly hunted herself as fair game that she accepts marriage with bland acquiescence as the obvious end of all feminine pursuits and all feminine existence.

CHAPTER IX.

IN DUCAL CIRCLES.

No true woman will ever believe that a man can be in love with two of her sex at once ; she judges him by herself, for a woman's love is always truly monogamic. So Linda, being quite certain in her own heart that Basil Maclaine admired and liked her very much indeed, had few qualms, if any, when he came home night after night and told her, in the simplicity of his British Philistine soul, how well he got on with Bertie Montgomery and the rich Miss Venables. She regarded them both, in fact, as standing for him in the same line ; it was one of Basil's little weaknesses. She knew he liked to be mixed up with that sort of people. Linda would laugh at it all to herself in her own dignified way, but she loved Basil too well ever seriously to doubt him for one moment, for all that.

So she took no heed of his frequent visits to Hurst Croft, or of his openly-expressed admiration for the heiress's beauty.

As to Bertie Montgomery, Basil Maclaine and he were quite sworn friends now. It was easy enough for any man to scrape acquaintance with Bertie Montgomery if he cared to do it. Basil went to see him frequently at the Die and Hazard, and on one such occasion, when a well-known plunger offered to cut the Duke's brother at cards three times running for a tenner a cut, Bertie Montgomery, not having that sum about him at the moment (as he airily explained), condescended to borrow three ten-pound notes in succession with easy nonchalance from his new friend, each of which he lost straight off on the turn of a card to his valorous opponent. Basil was somewhat disconcerted a few minutes later, however, after Bertie had left the room for a game of billiards, when the plunger, smiling broadly, remarked to him in a very confidential tone, 'I say, I didn't like to hint at it before Montgomery just now, though I tried to give you a friendly tip with my eye, but you oughtn't to have lent him thirty quid like that, you know. You'll never see the colour of your money again. He's not a bad sort of chap, Bertie ain't, if you take him in the right way; but he's got a beastly short memory where coin's concerned. As sure as eggs is eggs, he'll forget all about it.'

'You don't mean to say so!' Basil answered, taken aback.

'Oh yes, I do, though,' the plunger replied, with a sagacious nod. 'Runs in the family, don't you know. It's the blood that does it. Duke's just the same. Always see the money posted when you bet with Powysland. That's why he has to play nothing but roulette now. No private person cares to put his own good hard gold against Powysland's word or Powysland's paper. At a public table, it's all money down; and that's why he can only get any fun as things stand at present in the Casino at Monte Carlo or the Cercles at Homburg.'

Even so, however, Basil Maclaine didn't wholly grudge those thirty pounds. It was something to have bound one's self by ties of unexhausted pecuniary gratitude to the heir-presumptive of a dukedom, like Bertie Montgomery. For the present Duke, though married, was childless, as Basil had discovered by reference to the peerage on the evening of his first meeting with the next successor to the strawberry leaves; and Basil was not the man to grudge even thirty pounds, well spent in cementing a desirable friendship with the Very Best People.

Time flies, and the day of the pastoral play arrived at last. Basil got leave of absence for that afternoon from the head of the office. A mighty gathering of the dwellers in great houses among the Surrey hills assembled on the lawn at Hurst Croft, and money to the extent of several millions was represented, as Hubert Harrison ironically remarked, among the young ladies who sat on the front benches to witness the performance. Happily, the meteorological office favoured the event. According to Mr. Robert Scott, an anti-cyclone brooded over North-western Europe. 'Variable airs and calms: fair, warm, brighter,' ran the official forecast with its accustomed laconic brevity; and fair and warm and bright it was, indeed, that afternoon on the velvety slope of the downs near Leatherhead.

Everything went off as well as it could go. The open-air theatre had put on its very best scenery and properties for the grand occasion. The shade of the great spreading beeches and the dark gloom of the yews made the poet's ideal Arden live again visibly before the eyes of the spectators. Thrushes and linnets sang emulous from the elms to drown the noise of their human rivals. Sabine Venables, as Rosalind, looked a picture to behold; and Hubert Harrison, as the philosophic Jaques, seemed as poetically melancholy as the part demanded of him. Basil Maclaine's fantastic Touchstone had wit and lightness beyond what anybody expected; he had caught the very 'false gallop of verse,' and made all his points with practised skill and ease, being perhaps more applauded than anybody else in the whole entertainment. When all was over, and Sabine, coming up in her page's dress, congratulated him on his success and praised his elocution, he felt that at last he was really scoring. He said a pretty thing or two in reply, with distinguished readiness, and Sabine, accustomed to sitting at the receipt of pretty things as her natural due, accepted them so graciously that he began to think Bertie Montgomery was nowhere now, and that he himself was in the front running for the great heiress's hand and heart and fortune.

If there was a hitch in the proceedings

anywhere, it arose from the fact that the Celia was almost too frightened to speak her part; but as nobody was particularly interested in Celia, Basil said to himself, except Mr. Venables, that really was a point of very small importance.

The peculiarity of private theatricals is that they take six weeks at least to prepare for, and are over at last in two short hours. They leave, as a rule, an aching void behind them.

After the play was done, indeed, the company dispersed itself aimlessly about among the trees, and formed little groups beneath the shade of the imagined Arden, to discuss the actors, who mingled among them incongruously enough in the dresses they had worn in the course of the performance. One such group gathered round Old Affability himself, who, standing near the Italian terrace, with his hands behind his back, was loud in his praise of Woodbine Weatherley's Celia. 'The prettiest bit of acting in all the piece,' he observed warmly, 'and, in my opinion, the most thoroughly artistic.'

'Except Miss Venables',' Basil put in with a quiet smile. 'Her Rosalind was—what shall I say?—well, just Shakespeare's.'

'Yes, my daughter was good,' the typical British Philistine admitted candidly; 'she played her part well: she'd been admirably coached; but for native soul and reflectiveness, I must confess I prefer Miss Weatherley.'

As Mrs. Bouverie-Barton showed a disposition to contest this point at her accustomed length—she had 'views' on the drama—Basil Maclaine slipped off carelessly to a second group, who were talking near the tent about some case of suicide reported as the passing 'mystery' in that morning's papers. Bertie Montgomery stood here, and so did the two Harrisons. 'For my part,' Hubert was saying, as the civil servant sauntered up to join the group, 'I think the man behaved most abominably. If he wanted to kill himself, he might at least have taken the trouble to leave a note behind and tell us why he did it, so as to exculpate others. For a fellow to commit suicide, and leave it in doubt whether he wasn't murdered, is a gross injustice to many innocent people.'

'Oh, hang it all, Harrison!' Bertie Montgomery interposed, lighting a cigarette as he spoke, 'you're too down upon him altogether, poor old broken-down wretch! Why should he go and try to bring disgrace on his family? For my part, I think he acted quite right; and when *I* commit suicide, as I shall do some day, I suppose, like all the rest of us, when luck goes against me too hard, I'm not going to leave a scrap of paper behind me to incriminate myself and satisfy other people's curiosity. I'll let 'em guess who did it, as much as they like; and if they can't find out, why, then they may whistle for it. . . . Talking of whistles, I don't mind if I wet mine after all this thirsty Orlando business. Precious dry work, spouting in the open air.

Strains the voice so terribly. I'm as hoarse as a bull-frog. Any of you fellows come along to the tent and have a brandy split with me?'

Basil Maclaine was just going to volunteer for the honour of sharing the sub-ducal soda-water, when Charlie Simmons, by a rapid flank movement, got in before him, and walked off arm-in-arm towards the tent with Lord Adalbert. So Basil remained behind perforce to hear the rest of the colloquy, which degenerated forthwith into half a whisper as the two others disappeared under the big marquee. 'That was an unfortunate subject for Charlie to introduce just then,' Hubert Harrison said, in an undertone, as he looked askance after the two retreating young men, 'considering that Montgomery's father committed suicide himself, and never left a word or a line behind to say why he did it.'

'No, you don't mean that!' Basil exclaimed in surprise; 'I never heard of it.'

'Oh, it's well known to everybody!' Hubert went on, more openly. 'The way of the tribe. It's a family habit. Gambling and suicide are hereditary with the Montgomeries. Didn't you hear Lord Adalbert say himself, "Like all the rest of us?" They run through their money, and then they cut their throats. That's the regular routine. As soon as one's down the next man in succession marries an heiress again, gambles and drinks, and begins *da capo*. The minute her money's all gone, or he's tired of her or jealous of her—the same old game again, cut throat and exit.'

As he spoke he was interrupted by a late guest, just down from town to dine at Hurst Croft, with the very freshest news, hot from press, in his pocket.

'Seen this, Harrison?' the new-comer asked, holding out an evening paper in his hand as he spoke. 'Latest thing out this evening. Surprised to see Montgomery's here, all the same. He can't have heard it.

Somebody or other 'll have to break the news to him.'

All the bystanders crowded round and stared hard at the sheet over one another's shoulders. There it was, to be sure, in the very biggest and darkest of leaded type:

'Fourth Edition.—Suicide of a Nobleman. Unhappy End of the Duke of Powysland.'

Hubert Harrison read it out aloud for the benefit of the party:—'Homburg, July 20th, 11 a.m.—The Duke of Powysland was found dead in his bed here this morning, with his throat cut and the jugular vein severed. Nothing exact is known with regard to the circumstances as yet, but as the Duke's affairs were in a very embarrassed and encumbered state, it is generally believed he must have committed suicide. No papers or writing of any sort have been found in his room, but a hasty medical examination suggests the idea that the deceased nobleman must have inflicted the wound himself by means of a razor.'

'Later.—It is now almost certain that the Duke of Powysland deliberately took his own life, as the police find on inquiry he purchased the razor in person late last night at a well-known cutler's in the town of Homburg.'

There was silence for a moment, then a babel of voices. Everybody pressed forward to discuss the unseasonable news. In the midst of it all, Lord Adalbert and his satellite, refreshed from the tent, strolled up once more to know the cause of this sudden commotion. At the same moment, Old Affability himself, attracted by the obvious marks of profound interest, came down to join them. One or two of the guests made a hasty movement, as if to hide for the moment the disconcerting paper. But Lord Adalbert saw through their flimsy attempt at once. 'What is it?' he cried, flinging himself upon the group with some excitement, and holding out his hand for the print they were trying to conceal from him. 'Anything wrong at

Homburg? Eh? Powysland been making a stupid fool of himself?'

Hubert Harrison held out the paper in reply with a significant gesture. 'There is something very wrong indeed at Homburg,' he answered in a warning voice. 'The Duke has been hurt, seriously hurt; you can look for yourself if you like and see it.'

Lord Adalbert took the sheet with a very pale face. As he read, his cheeks grew whiter and even whiter. At last he handed it back with trembling fingers. 'I thought so,' he said, in a profoundly sobered voice. 'At last he's done it.'

Mr. Venables, in his turn, received the paper from his guest's hands. As soon as he had hastily glanced over the telegram, he turned round to the young man with an irreproachable face of conventional condolence. 'Your grace would like to retire awhile,' he said deferentially. 'This news has been too much for you. Will you come into the house for the present, till the shock is over, and you've had time to realize it?'

'No, thank you,' the young man answered, steadying himself for support against one of the garden seats. 'This is very sudden. Very sudden indeed. But not, for all that, wholly unexpected. I think perhaps I'd better go back to town at once. I've not myself alone to think of. I must break it to my mother.'

He spoke with genuine feeling, and tears stood in his eyes. That was only natural. Blood, with all of us, is thicker than water. Mr. Venables looked at him with profound interest. 'Thomas,' he cried, turning sharply round to one of the servants, 'run to the stables, quick. Tell Bridges to bring up the landau at once, to take the Duke of Powysland down to the station.'

At the sound of that title, so lately his brother's, now for the first time his own, the new Duke looked up with a start of surprise. 'No, thank you,' he said once more. 'It's very kind of you, but I'd rather walk. Don't any of you fellows bother to come with me, please. I prefer to be alone. I mean what I say, Maclaine. I shall be obliged if you'll allow me to go by myself. It's taken my breath away for the moment, and I'd like to have time to collect my thoughts before I see my mother.'

He walked slowly across the lawn towards the winding carriage-drive that led down the hill. He was profoundly moved. But Old Affability, glancing after him with an admiring gaze as he went, murmured softly to himself, like one who gloats over a delicious morsel, 'It's made a Duke of him! What a singular coincidence! To think I should have been the first man in England ever to address him by his proper title as Duke of Powysland!'

CHAPTER X.

A THUNDERBOLT FALLS.

One by one the guests dispersed rapidly, this gloomy termination to the day's entertainment affording them a natural excuse for somewhat hasty leave-taking; and before long the Hurst Croft house-party were left almost by themselves, with the special exception of the one late guest, and of Hubert Harrison, both of whom had a long-standing engagement to stop to dinner. Bertie Montgomery was also to have been of the party, of course; but, under existing circumstances, his place must needs remain vacant.

Hubert strolled up with Sabine to the house. Mr. Venables followed at a little distance behind with Woodbine Weatherley.

The remaining guest took charge of Mrs. Walker. 'Papa's always so kind,' Sabine said, glancing back at her little friend with a patronizing air. 'Woodbine ought to have gone away from us to-night by rights—she was asked down for a fortnight—but papa wouldn't hear of letting her go so soon. He's so wonderfully considerate for girls in her position. He said she'd be tired out after the performance, and it would be sheer cruelty to send her back to that governesses' home place where she stops in London; she'd find it so dreary after the day's excitement.'

'He's very thoughtful, I know,' Hubert responded with a sigh.

'And it isn't as if she was pretty or attractive, either,' Sabine went on, musing. 'A poor, feeble little atomy of a girl like that! It's just pure goodness of heart. He's always been kind to Woodbine ever since she and I were at school together. She was a pale, frail little creature then, with no looks to boast of; and she'll be a frail, pale little creature as long as she lives, till they work her to death at some high school somewhere. She reads Herbert Spencer, and talks like a book about survival of the fittest; but she isn't fit to battle with the world herself; that's the long and short of it. Natural selection would select her outright to go to the wall. I wish to goodness some nice rich man would take a fancy to her instead, and marry her offhand. But that's not likely.'

'Offer her to the Duke,' Hubert suggested, with a sudden happy thought.

But Sabine shook her head. 'The Duke wants money,' she answered, with the precocious wisdom of the rather ripe girl brought up in the thick of society. 'He'll sell his title dear—dearer than ever now. He must have thousands and thousands to pay off old scores, and keep him going on the turf and at the Die and Hazard. And he'll get them, too, after this—get them as soon as he chooses to ask for them.'

'Where?' Hubert Harrison interposed pointedly.

Sabine Venables stared him back in the face with a stony stare. 'How should I know!' she answered in her most provoking style. 'I'm sure I can't say. Wherever he likes, I should think, Mr. Harrison.'

'Sabine! You mean it?'

His face turned deadly white. His heart stood still. Had the budding strawberry-leaves produced such an effect upon her already?

Sabine Venables started too, the change in his colour was so marked and so instantaneous. It pained her to see him. She was ashamed of her own coquettish caprice. 'Hubert,' she said faintly, in a very low voice, 'how can you ever ask me? You might know . . . I love you.'

'You admit it?' he cried, overjoyed. 'Oh, Sabine, you admit it?'

'Take care, silly boy!' Sabine answered, repenting once more her unwonted relentment.

'Papa's just behind. If you stare at me like that, he'll guess what we're talking about.'

'But you can't unsay it,' Hubert exclaimed, all tremulous with delight. 'You can never unsay it. With your own lips you've told me plainly you love me. When a woman once tells you that, she tells you all. As long as I live, I shall have it always to remember.'

'Well, don't put it in the *Boomerang*, anyhow,' Sabine retorted provokingly. 'That's the worst of telling anything to one of you writing people, you know: one's sure to see it staring one in the face in print before one knows it almost.'

'But, Sabine, I shall put something some day in the *Boomerang*, now you've told me you love me,' the young man said, exulting. 'I shall put it before very long, too, if I have my own way. "We understand that a marriage has been arranged between——"'

Sabine cut him short with an imperious gesture. 'What do you mean?' she cried proudly, her eyes blazing fire at his bare suggestion. 'I never gave you any ground to suppose *that*, did I? I said I loved you. That was a foolish confession—just to keep you quiet. But I never said I'd marry you. Do you think because a woman loves a man she's bound to chuck away all her chances, offhand, of becoming a Duchess?'

'Sabine,' the young man put in, glancing back at her with admiration, 'you do yourself an injustice. In your heart I know you never seriously thought such a thought as that. You say it only just to tease me and make me uncomfortable.'

Sabine's proud lips relented once more. She was a strange compound. 'Hubert,' she answered, looking up at him in return with a certain confiding womanly pride, 'you're the only man on earth who ever understands me. I believe that's the reason I—er—like you so much. *You* can read what I mean. The other men never know one little bit what I'm driving at.'

'Then you mean to consent to——'

Sabine shook her head decisively. 'I mean nothing of the sort,' she replied with quiet reserve. 'I only mean I'm in a sort of a kind of a way rather fond of you. I'm not going to make up my mind just yet. I shall play with my mouse a bit longer, I can tell you, before I decide whether or not I shall kill it or let it go.' And she looked up at him once more with a teasing smile, like an Egyptian Pasht, in her wayward spoilt fashion. 'Or, rather,' she added, after a telling pause, 'with both my mice—one of them a Duke, and the other a commoner.'

And that was all Hubert Harrison, for all his cleverness, could manage to get out of her.

At dinner, the conversation not unnaturally turned for the most part upon the new Duke and his unexpected elevation to the honours and glories of the British peerage.

'He'll marry before long, I should think,' Old Affability remarked, in the course of dessert, turning a beaming countenance successively round on all the members of the company. ‘ A man in his position is pretty sure to marry. And quite right, too. He ought to, I say. Keep up the family line—pity to see a good old name die out. His brother, the late Duke, was married also—but without issue, of course, as I see from Debrett. Without issue.’

‘ Who did he marry ?’ Sabine asked languidly. She was much too unaffected to say primly ‘ whom,’ as some purists would have wished her to do.

‘ An heiress, of course,’ Hubert put in with a meaning smile. ‘ A Miss Foster, of Dublin, last of a long line of wealthy whisky-distillers.’

Sabine shuddered with her pretty bare shoulders in her evening dress. ‘ What people these peers will get in with !’ she cried with a little pout. ‘ Anything on earth for money ! I declare it disgusts one.’

‘ My dear !’ her father exclaimed, with a

faintly disapproving frown. 'Distilling's an exceedingly gentlemanly business. Almost as much so, in fact, as banking or brewing.' Being a banker himself, the typical British Philistine had a nice appreciation of the relative social values of mercantile enterprise.

'And the distiller's daughter had no children?' Sabine asked, to turn the thread of the talk, which she felt showed symptoms of almost growing personal.

'No children!' Hubert echoed with an affirmative nod. 'Else Lord Adalbert wouldn't this moment be Duke of Powysland.'

'Heiresses very seldom *do* have children,' Woodbine Weatherley ventured to interpose innocently, in a frightened way. 'People should never marry them. Mr. Galton says in his book on heredity it's because they're the last surviving members of a decadent stock which has exhausted its energies in the constant effort of money-making. I suppose he's right. He has a lot of cases in his book to prove it, I remember.'

Sabine laughed outright at the malapropos remark. And certainly, as Hubert Harrison glanced from one girl to the other, he felt there was nothing that looked very ostentatiously decadent about Sabine Venables. But Old Affability, to his immense surprise, didn't resent the unintentional imputation upon the money-making type. Hubert took it as one more proof of the unobtrusive goodness about which Sabine had spoken. Indeed, the typical British Philistine showed surprising tact in rescuing his little guest from her unhappy position. 'For my part,' he said genially, 'if I were a young man looking out for a wife, peer or no peer, what would take *me* most would be neither face nor figure, but the Intellectual Graces. That's what seems to me most important in a woman—the Intellectual Graces. Beauty fades, and prettiness palls on one, and youth passes away like—er—like the flower on the grass; but the Intellectual Graces continue for ever. They never wear out. They improve with age. What I should go in for decidedly is the Intellectual Graces.' And after this unwonted flight into the Higher Regions of Thought, Old Affability raised his glass of claret between his finger and thumb, and looked through it fixedly for some seconds at the electric light that glowed and flickered above the orchid-decked dinner-table.

'Fiddlesticks!' Sabine responded, crushing him at once, though Woodbine Weatherley gazed at her in hushed amazement. 'Dukes don't want intellectual graces, I'm sure. What *they* want is money—money, money, money, money—and plenty of it.'

Her father's glance came down at a rush to earth from heaven. 'I—I wasn't thinking of Dukes, my dear,' he replied shortly, gazing across at her with fatherly affection and pride. 'A Duke, I suppose, if in straightened circumstances for one of his rank, should ally himself to a person who can enable him properly to keep up his position in the country. I've not a word to say against that. I—er—I concur in it, and approve of it. I was thinking rather of men in the middle ranks of life. I believe a person, in such a case, even if conscious of not being particularly brilliant or particularly intellectual himself, often admires brilliancy and intellect in others. And where that is so, he should marry where he finds it. If the possessor will overlook his shortcomings and take him, he should marry where he finds it.'

'Woodbine dear,' Sabine remarked coldly, catching her friend's eye, 'shall we leave papa and Mr. Harrison to discuss this very interesting and instructive question together?' And with a curl of her lip and a faint glance at Hubert she swept out of the room, her train a yard behind, driving poor meek little Woodbine like a lamb before her.

That evening, when all the rest had gone, the typical English Philistine stood nervously for a moment with his hand on the drawing-room mantelpiece, and stared hard at Sabine, in a curiously preoccupied and hesitating manner, as was often his wont when Argentines were declining.

'Well?' Sabine asked at last, seeing he had apparently something unpleasant to communicate. 'What is it, papa? Great fall in Turks? Crédit Foncier going down? What do you stand staring at me like that for, I wonder?'

Her father started, and glanced around him uneasily. 'Oh, nothing!' he answered, in an apologetic voice. 'Nothing at all. Nothing. Nothing. Nothing. Market's firm as a rock. But, Sabine, I just wanted to ask you—I have a particular reason—*did* Lord Adalbert—the Duke, I mean—did he —er—say anything particular to you this afternoon when the play was ended?'

'He said he thought everything had gone off better than he expected,' Sabine answered with a smile. 'He didn't expect it to go off as well as he expected, which may have been his notion of saying something funny;

yet there's a deal of truth in it, too, if you have the trick to understand it.'

'Well, but besides that?' her father urged, eyeing her hard. 'You know what I mean, Sabine. Did he say anything of a sort that might lead you to suppose——'

Sabine shook her head decisively. 'He never said a word of a sort to lead me to suppose anything on earth—good, bad, or indifferent,' she replied in a hasty voice. 'I know what you mean, of course, however you blink it, and I don't mind answering you point blank, if it comes to that. He didn't propose to me.'

'Sabine, my dear child!' the typical British Philistine ejaculated in pained surprise, almost shocked at such unmaidenly plainness of speech and directness of purpose. 'How *can* you talk so?'

'Nary propose!' Sabine went on maliciously, the wicked pleasure of shocking her father taking possession of her, body and soul, as that particular devil will take possession of us all under similar conditions. 'And what's more, I don't believe he ever means to. Buyers are shy, as you say on the Stock Exchange. He won't come up to the scratch, that's what's the matter with him. He dawdles and nibbles around, and looks at the bait from every side, but he can't be induced to take a good solid bite at it, so that one could hook him and land him outright if one really wanted to.'

Mr. Venables was too profoundly distressed in soul at such recklessness to answer for a moment. Then he said slowly, 'This is very unfortunate. I thought he'd be sure to speak to you to-day. He would have spoken, too, if it hadn't been for that most ill-timed interruption of the telegram about his brother. I—I wish, Sabine, he hadn't heard of it—his accession to the title, I mean—till *after* he'd had a chance of speaking to you alone on the subject. Now that he's a Duke, you see, perhaps he'll think——'

'Sir!'

Mr. Venables retreated into his shell at once, like a snail whose horns have been touched with a sharp prickle. Sabine stood glaring at him across the mantelpiece in angry pride. Did he mean to insinuate—did he dare to insinuate—that a Duke or any other living creature on earth could for a moment consider himself too highly placed a match for Sabine Venables? If so, she could never permit such a slight to her pride, even from her own father.

There was a moment's pause. Then Mr. Venables intervened once more with tentative hesitation. 'I had a special reason for wishing him to . . . er . . . to make any propositions on the subject he might have to suggest . . . before taking a certain step myself to which I attach a certain amount of importance in this respect. To tell you the truth, Sabine, I've been delaying the step in question too long, very much against my will, in order to give him time to come to the point; and I've done so at a considerable cost of personal inconvenience. But matters now have taken a different turn.' Mr. Venables drew himself up very stiff, glanced sharply at his daughter, and then regarded his own clean-shaven face and spotless white choker in the mirror-panel of the overmantel. 'They took a different turn this afternoon,' he went on with obvious embarrassment. 'And therefore, now the young man's a Duke, I shall give him just another fortnight to make up his mind in—after which time, if he hasn't—er—placed things upon a satisfactory basis for all parties concerned, I shall—well, I shall proceed at once to take my own course in the matter without waiting any longer for him to declare himself.'

Sabine gazed back at her father in speechless amazement. A vague, blank terror seized upon her mind. What on earth could he mean by this enigmatical pronouncement? 'I don't understand you,' she gasped out feebly, sinking back into a chair. 'You don't mean to say you'll—you'll actually offer me as a present to any man!'

It was Mr. Venables' turn to look surprised now. 'God bless the child!' he exclaimed with a bewildered stare, 'what on earth is she talking about? Goodness gracious me! I wasn't speaking about *you* at all, Sabine. I was speaking about myself. Under all the circumstances, unless the Duke proposes within a fortnight, I won't any longer delay the public announcement of my own intentions.'

'*What* intentions?' Sabine gasped out once more, growing faint with the horror of that unknown presentiment.

'My intentions as to my future,' Mr. Venables went on, still gazing abstractedly into the glass, and pulling up his shirt collar with an approving air. 'I was anxious to put off announcing them to the world as long as possible, in order not to interfere with your prospects of settlement in life; but after what has taken place to-day, I really don't see how I can put it off any longer.'

Sabine arose once more and staggered towards him wildly. The words stuck in her throat. She could hardly get them out. 'Oh, father! father!' she cried, holding both hands to her head as if to keep it from splitting, 'you don't mean *that!* You can't mean *that!* You can never mean to tell me you're going to get married!'

She said it in a fierce outburst of utter despair. She couldn't believe it was possible. It was too, too terrible. It rose up before her only as a mad, incredible nightmare. He could never, never, never mean *that*. Whatever his strange, problematical words might portend, it could never be anything quite so horrible, so crushing, so annihilating!

Mr. Venables gazed in the glass once more, and stroked his smooth chin, as who should say, 'Why not, indeed? Am I not as young and good-looking as any man of sixty can reasonably expect to be?' Then he answered slowly, and with some deliberation as to the choice of his words, 'Well, I certainly *have* of late contemplated that course; and this afternoon I took a step which renders it now partially inevitable. I was betrayed by my feelings of admiration into saying, quite impromptu—on the spur of the moment—a few words I had meant, if possible, to postpone till later.'

'To whom?' Sabine cried faintly, clutching at a chair. 'Not Mrs. Bouverie-Barton?'

Mr. Venables glanced back at her in profound astonishment. 'I'm surprised you should ask me such a question,' he answered, raising his eyebrows by slow degrees as he took in the full implications of his daughter's ignorance. 'And you a girl, too, with all their talk about woman's intuitions! Why, who on earth could it be of our acquaintance, except one peerless person? Who on earth else has those Intellectual Graces which one looks for so incontestably in the woman one loves? Who on earth could you think of naming in the same day with her, I wonder? Surely I need hardly tell you it's—Woodbine Weatherley.'

CHAPTER XI.

TWO SIDES TO A QUESTION.

Sabine Venables never closed her eyes that whole night long. She lay awake in her bed, hour after hour, in silent misery, thinking over all that this terrible avowal enclosed of humiliation and shame for her. She was a proud-natured girl, and her father's announcement had burst upon her with such a sudden blinding force of dismay and horror that she hardly knew as yet how she could ever outlive it.

And, indeed, she had reason, for she could scarcely realize at the first blush herself what a total change it meant in her position and prospects.

In the first place, there was the mere

primary fact of the stepmother. Sabine Venables shared that common feminine prejudice. It's very unreasonable, to be sure, that girls should object to their fathers doing the very thing they themselves spend their entire time in endeavouring to compass; but such is nevertheless the usual instinct of female humanity; a girl feels it almost a personal slight and insult to herself that her father should dream of taking a new head for his household. And Woodbine, too, of all girls in the world! That poor shrinking little atomy she had so pitied and patronized; to think that Woodbine, enthroned in state, in her stead, was to pose henceforth as mistress of Hurst Croft, and that she herself, Sabine Venables, the admired, the petted, would have to play second fiddle in future to a pallid, hollow-cheeked, consumptive-looking little nursery governess—to walk after her in to dinner, to stand at her beck and call in the paternal drawing-room, to sit on the front seat, with her back to the horses, when they drove out together with her father in the park, to nestle under her protecting wing as the obedient stepdaughter at dances and parties! it was too, too degrading.

But that was not all. Worse depths yet loomed behind. Dimly and unconsciously at first, more definitely afterwards, as she recovered strength to face that blinding blow, Sabine saw that Woodbine's elevation to the first post at Hurst Croft meant nothing less than her own definitive though gradual deposition from her throne as heiress. She was almost too proud to acknowledge in her own mind the full degradation involved for her in that painful come-down in life. It hit her hard on her tenderest susceptibilities. She knew she was beautiful; she knew she was attractive; she knew she was rich; she knew she was made much of wherever she went; but she had never had any reason till that moment to try in her own mind the difficult task of separating herself from her father's money-bags, of deciding how much of the admiration and adulation lavished upon her was due to her own wit, sprightliness, or beauty, and how much to the inheritance of the famous Venables' banking interest in the City. Now she would be put to the humiliating necessity of facing that problem in practical life. She would find out before long, by her admirers' behaviour under these altered circumstances, what proportion of their homage was due to Sabine Venables herself, viewed as a human being, and what proportion was due to the prospective heiress of Hurst Croft estate with its correlative thousands.

To so proud a soul the bare idea that the change could make any difference in her position at all was painful to recognise. Even to herself, it humiliated her to acknowledge it. She would have liked to think all this attention bestowed upon her was her guerdon as a woman; she hated the necessity for having her eyes opened to the probable fact that a very large part of it was due merely to the reflex of her father's balance.

And yet, from the very first moment she fully appreciated—in a way—the immensity of the downfall, and the potentialities of the situation. If Woodbine gave her father (now ten years a widower) an heir for Hurst Croft, her humiliation would be complete. She would sink at once to be only the rich man's residuary legatee. Instead of being sought after as the best match of the season, she would drop into the position of a mere target for younger sons whose modest expectations of catches were easily satisfied. Where prospective Dukes and Marquises had been wont to pay assiduous court to the fantastic heiress, an occasional honourable (probably the youngest scion of an Irish peerage in the Encumbered Estates Court) would hint henceforth the possibility of his accepting her, if approved, with a sufficient dowry to support him in unassuming idleness. To come down to that would be hateful to Sabine Venables' haughty spirit. She didn't wish to be taken as a modest competence. She must be wooed like a queen, if they wanted at all to woo her.

Not that Sabine really and truly cared twopence, in her heart of hearts, for all these upholsteries and gewgaws of life that Old Affability esteemed at so high a valuation. If Bertie Montgomery had proposed to her the day before, she would have kept him dangling about for half an hour, playing with him (in her own words) as a cat plays with a mouse, and then would have told him in very plain terms that, much as she thanked him for the honour he had done her in singling her out to assist in the repair of the dilapidated Powysland fortunes, and the refurbishment of the shabby Powysland mansions, she regretted she didn't like him one quarter enough ever to dream of marrying him. What she would miss in life now would be—the chance of saying as much to other men in future. Even if you don't want to kill anybody, says the Roman moralist in a famous line, it's a pleasure to feel you have it in your power to kill him. And even if Sabine Venables didn't want to marry a Duke, it was a pleasure to her, at least, to feel in her heart she had it in her power, if she willed, to refuse him.

She had grown so accustomed to that atmosphere, indeed, that she hardly knew how she could breathe any other. Nay, it was partly for that reason (though she was scarcely conscious of it to herself) that she kept Hubert Harrison so long at bay, torturing him with doubts, and teasing him with petty concessions, while she dangled the grapes temptingly all the time before his eyes, and withdrew them in a coquettish pet whenever he thought he was just going at last to really grasp them. She loved Hubert; till that moment, she had never told herself unreservedly how much she loved him; but she had delayed letting him know the fact too plainly, because she couldn't bear to tear herself away all at once from her admiring coterie of courtesy lords and actual baronets. She didn't want to burn her boats behind her; she didn't want to abdicate and renounce her kingdom. If she had married Hubert, as she always figured to herself she meant to do, in her own heart, at the end of the chapter, why, that chapter at least would be ended, ended for ever, and with it all the excitement and extorted homage of a coquette's free period of unrestricted flirtation. As Mrs. Hubert Harrison she would still have filled an important place in society, of course, and would have made Hubert rich and happy, and got him into Parliament, and all that sort of thing, and settled down to be a happy mother of children; but she would no longer be able to sway her little court of obedient suitors with the same absolute, not to say unreasoning, rule, as when she flitted before their eyes a potential and possible Duchess of Powysland.

And now, in the dead hours of the night, as she lay there with burning cheeks and tearless eyes — for she couldn't cry, poor child! her pride wouldn't let her—she felt that all these bubbles had burst for ever, and that she might sink before long to be as nobody in the house before the face of Woodbine Weatherley's prospective infant. How she hated, in her heart, that hypothetical atom of non-existent humanity! If she married Hubert at all, she must marry him now, as comparatively poor; for supposing a boy were borne—and to that stroke of fate Sabine resigned her soul in patience immediately—papa, of course, would leave him everything, or almost everything—people of papa's sort always do leave things so; their great idea in life is to become the founder of a family (what gross injustice!), and then all the world would say, in chorus, she'd taken Hubert at last as a *pis aller*, because she found she couldn't catch the Duke of Powysland. That abyss was too profound—from a Duke to a penny-a-liner! Yet that was what all the world would say, she felt sure; and, recognising it, she hardly knew how she could ever bring herself, much as she loved him, to marry Hubert.

Ah, how differently things had turned out, in the blind caprice of fate, from what she dreamt and intended! Her own idea had been that, after refusing Bertie Montgomery and half a dozen other equally brilliant offers, she would turn round, before the face of the world, and poor scandalized papa—how she loved to shock him!—and say boldly, 'No, thank you, none of your coronets for me! I prefer to take the man after my own heart. I might have been a Duchess; I choose, rather, to marry Hubert Harrison!' That would have been immense! That would have been delicious! That would have been noble! That would have been beautiful! That would have combined romance in real life with the sense of social triumph dear to the female heart, especially when built on Sabine Venables' pattern. And now—she could hardly bear to think of it, it was so lame a conclusion. To marry Hubert Harrison, as things stood at present, would almost in a sense look like seeming to put up with him.

To put up with Hubert! That king of men! And she so loved and admired him! He. was so kind and so clever; he understood her so perfectly. She loved to listen to him as he talked after dinner with the poor creatures around him; she loved to hear what people said about those brilliant things of his in the morning papers, which must lead him one day straight into the House of Commons. For Hubert's sake, she would readily have given up a whole round dozen of Bertie Montgomerys. It would have made her feel so proud to say to Hubert, 'My darling, my darling! they may ask me till all's blue; but I love you ten thousand times better than all the Dukes in Christendom.' And as things stood to-night, she could never, never, never say it.

It was an endless night; but, like all things endless, at last it ended.

When she got up in the morning, her head

ached. At breakfast, she was coldly polite to Woodbine. Whatever else people said, they should never say she forgot her dignity in her endeavours to secure some portion of the new favourite's countenance or of her father's fortune. If she fell, she would fall, like Clarendon, with honour. Nobody should ever be able to accuse her of having truckled to the governess girl her father selected. To her, Woodbine should always be merely 'Mrs. Venables.'

After breakfast, Sabine went off into the library alone. It was hateful to her to face that deceitful, designing creature. She was angry with Woodbine. During the night she had harboured many hard thoughts against her. That this feeble little image, a mere Girton adventuress, should have wormed her way into the house, and into papa's affections, by playing upon the absurd vanity and conceit of a man old enough to be her own father, in order to get his money and cheat herself, Sabine, out of her natural inheritance—oh !

no words were too bad for it. She was a wretch, a criminal! If it had been any other man on earth, Sabine could almost have forgiven her; but Thorndyke Venables! oh, really too ridiculous! Papa was a very nice man in his way, of course, viewed as a father; but, that at his present age, and with his paternal habits, after ten years of celibate life, any woman under fifty should ever dream of marrying him, or, rather, of selling herself to him (for it could be nothing but that)—pah! the very thought of it shocked and disgusted her. Woodbine had sunk below zero in her estimation. She could hardly manage through breakfast to be frigidly polite to her.

She seated herself in an arm-chair, and pretended to begin reading the *Morning Post*. The words swam before her eyes illegibly, of course, but that didn't matter. It gave her some ostensible reason for sitting there alone. Presently there came a timid little knock at the door. The sound annoyed Sabine beyond expression. Such infamous vulgarity!

What did the person who made it mean by knocking? So exceedingly ill-bred! Didn't she know that in a gentleman's house nobody ever knocks at the door of any reception-room? If that was the new under-house-maid's idea of her duty, Sabine said to herself savagely, she'd speak to her upon the subject. Or, rather, she added to herself with a bitter little smile, she'd ask the future Mrs. Venables, in anticipation of her coming reign, to offer a few appropriate words of advice to her.

'Come in!' she answered, as one answers a servant, and sat pretending still to be absorbed in that interesting *cause célèbre*.

'Sabine!' a little voice said piteously and pleadingly by her side. It was a very small voice, and its tones were enough to disarm a tiger.

'Oh, it's you, is it?' Sabine answered, looking up unconcernedly. 'I thought it was Julia, and I was going to ask you (as it's more your place than mine) to tell her that *nobody* ever knocks at all at a downstairs door—any door but a bedroom, I mean—in anything better than a tradesman's family.

Woodbine turned her eyes towards her imperious friend with an imploring look. 'Forgive me, Sabine dear,' she cried, flinging herself passionately upon the tall girl's neck, and taking both hands in hers as she kissed them a dozen times over. 'I saw by your manner at breakfast that Mr. Venables had told you all; and I couldn't help observing that you were very, very angry with me. And just now I asked him, and he said he had, and he was afraid it had hurt you, and it had made him so wretched. And, oh! Sabine, I know exactly how you feel; I sympathize with you so much; but when he asked me last night—my dear, my dear, what on earth could I answer?'

A great red spot burnt in Sabine's cheek as she drew herself up and replied slowly, 'You could have said that no money on earth would ever tempt you to do anything so mean, so heartless, or so wicked.'

Woodbine fell upon her friend's lap and sobbed in an agony of misery. 'Oh, Sabine!' she cried, 'I haven't slept a wink all night, wondering how you'd feel and what you'd say to it; and I was horribly afraid of the effect it might produce upon you. But anything as bad as *this*, oh! I never dreamt of it.'

'You've brought it upon yourself,' Sabine answered, unmoved, with the stern virtue of retributive justice. 'If you'd had a spark of womanly pride, or honesty, or shame in your nature, you could never have accepted him. I didn't mean to say it to you; I meant to leave you to your own conscience; but when you come here asking me for my forgiveness and my sympathy almost—*me*, whom you've insulted, and disgraced, and supplanted—I can't help speaking out, Woodbine. I can't help it. I can't help it.'

'Sabine!' Woodbine cried once more,

raising up her face in her agony, and confronting even those terrible angry black eyes of hers; 'I thought of you before I answered him; I thought more than once of you; for weeks before, ever since it first occurred to me he might perhaps be going to ask me—ever since I began to notice how gentle and kind he was—I said to myself over and over again fervently, "Even if he asks me, for Sabine's sake it's my duty to refuse him." I meant to refuse him all along, even yesterday afternoon, when the play was over.' She paused and hesitated. 'It was as you and Mr. Harrison were walking up from the ground,' she went on; 'Mr. Venables lingered behind with me, and congratulated me on my acting, and was so very, very sweet and good to me. And he took me quite by surprise. When he asked me, I faltered. I wanted to say No—I thought I ought to say No—but somehow I couldn't, couldn't frame my lips to say it. Sabine, Sabine, my own heart wouldn't let me. I thought of you; but he pleaded so hard. And even then I didn't. I held my lips tight, though my heart went fast; but he saw what I thought, dear. And he slipped *this* on my finger before I could make up my mind to falter out *No*. And then he smiled and said I had accepted him.'

'Well, there's still time to undeceive him, before he becomes the laughing-stock of the county,' Sabine answered coldly. 'Sooner than I'd marry a man for his money—and a man twice one's own age, too—I'd cut off my right hand, or I'd starve in the gutter. Money or title, I'd despise them both, unless love went with them. Do you think I'd marry that wretched Montgomery man, for example, just because he's a Duke? Why, sooner than take him, I'd die an old maid; I'd work my fingers to the bone, and take in washing. I know you're poor, and too weak to work, and unable to earn your own living, and all that, and I'd make every allowance for you; but sooner than marry a man for board and lodging and a roof over my head,

I'd—I'd sell flowers at a crossing, and die of consumption at last in a hospital. If you wanted help or befriending, you know I'd have given it you; but that you should come into my own house—you, such an innocent-looking girl as you are, that one would think butter wouldn't melt in your mouth—and then set yourself to work to steal my father's heart away from me, and marry him for a home—oh! I call it despicable. I call it despicable, despicable, despicable!'

Woodbine rose, and confronted her, all tearful, with a puzzled look of wonderment and of childish innocence. 'But, Sabine,' she cried pitifully, in a very earnest voice, 'I *do* so love him!'

Sabine drew back almost as if she had been stung. She could forgive Woodbine almost anything else save that; but not hypocrisy. 'Love him!' she repeated incredulously, with a scornful intonation. 'Love papa! Love him in *that* sort of way! Oh, Miss Weatherley, how ridiculous!'

Woodbine gazed hard into her face once more, with eyes more puzzled and surprised than ever. 'But I *do* love him, Sabine,' she cried. 'I love him with all my heart and soul. From the very first moment I ever saw him, almost, I loved him, oh—I loved him, I loved him, inexpressibly!'

Her voice had the genuine ring of truth in it, but what she said was too utterly incredible for Sabine to believe. The proud girl gazed, and wondered whether that poor feeble little atomy's head was going wrong somehow. Love poor papa with all her heart and soul! Such a man as papa! Oh, it was too, too comical.

'Why, Woodbine,' she said slowly, in a very cold voice, 'you *must* be joking.'

Woodbine flung herself upon the ground at Sabine's feet once more. 'No, no, dear,' she cried, laying her head in her friend's lap and hugging her knees nervously; 'I'm in earnest. I mean it. How could I ever help loving him? He's so good and so gentle.

Nobody else ever spoke to me on this earth as he's done. Nobody else ever understood me. Nobody else ever sympathized with me. He's talked to me till he's wormed his way deep into my heart, and I can't bear to leave him, I can't bear to go away from him. It made me so sad yesterday to think I must go. When he asked me last night, I had a hard struggle with myself. I said to myself, "For Sabine's sake I ought to say *No* to him." And then it flashed across me suddenly, like a great fierce pain, that if I said *No*, I should have to go away, and perhaps stay away for ever and ever from him. And I couldn't have borne that. It would have killed me outright. Oh, Sabine darling, I could never now live anywhere without him.'

Sabine looked down upon her with the wondering pity one bestows in an asylum upon some pathetic mania. The girl really meant it—she couldn't doubt that any longer. Woodbine, who acted so ill, could never in her life have acted like this! But, oh, how insane of her! Sabine couldn't see (for, like so many girls, though quick in passing intuition, she was lacking in any real depth of psychological insight into the minds of others very unlike herself) how natural it was that this feeble little stray should have fallen in love at first sight with the only living being who, in all her poor short life, had ever paid attention to her, sympathized with her, flattered her. She didn't see how natural it was that Woodbine should make much of such a man as Mr. Venables when he laid, as it were, all his honours and riches, a willing gift, at the feet of the poor little despised governess. She didn't see how natural it was for a shrinking, sensitive, affectionate soul to repose its confidence freely in the very first person who had ever shown the faintest desire to obtain it. 'Nobody else ever understood me,' she said. Why, that was just what Sabine herself thought about Hubert Harrison. The coincidence struck her. But, oh, what a difference! She wasn't psychologist enough to know herself that every woman who ever fell in love on this earth thinks just so about her own soul and the man who loves her.

Sabine gazed at her fixedly, and answered in a very chilly voice, 'It must be so, I suppose. You seem to be really capable of loving him—that way?'

The poor small thing raised her head once more with a pleading gesture. 'And I can never be happy,' she said, with her eyes dim with tears, 'till you've called me Woodbine again, and thrown your dear arms around me, and kissed me on my lips, and told me you've forgiven me. Oh, Sabine, I'll try never to stand in your way at all. But you *must* just kiss me and tell me you forgive me.'

Sabine looked down at those wistful eyes and that pale small face, and her resolution melted. 'You don't know how hard a trial you've put me to, my dear,' she answered slowly, 'but—there—I forgive you, Woodbine.' And bending down with an effort, she gave way and kissed her.

Woodbine flung herself upon her friend's neck, and burst into floods of passionate tears. 'Oh, thank you, dear!' she cried. 'Ten thousand times thank you. I shall be happy now!' And she sobbed as if her poor little heart would break for many minutes.

CHAPTER XII.

THE DUKE PLUNGES.

Before the fortnight was over—the fortnight Mr. Venables had allowed in his own mind for Sabine to settle herself in—the new-made Duke found his way once more down to Hurst Croft. He had his reasons for coming. Poor Powysland's affairs had now been 'cleared up,' as the lawyers phrase it—the dry light of legal day had at last been let in upon that endless complication of bills, and notes of hand, and mortgages, and gambling debts; but the result of the clearing was one which showed the balance of the estate so very much on the wrong side of the ledger that the new Duke made up his mind at once nothing was left for him now but to marry immediately.

To marry was, indeed, an imperative necessity. His lawyers were talking about 'equity of redemption.' Llanfyllin Castle itself was at stake this time; while Powysland House, in London, the last remnant of the old ducal splendour, had fallen into such a state of comparative decay that the Duke was really ashamed to meet the reproachful gaze of the family portraits. Nevertheless, as far as his own inclinations were concerned, the sacrifice was a painful one. Adalbert Montgomery was one of those butterfly bachelors who, in their own hateful and anti-social phrase, 'prefer their liberty.' He wanted to be free to do as he liked, for good or for evil—and especially for evil. Not that he was what people generally call a bad man; he was merely the average product of a bad system; he held that the world existed, so far as he was concerned, mainly for the purpose of giving him pleasure; and provided he got it, by hook or by crook, flitting from flower to flower, he cared very little what expense or trouble it entailed upon those mere outsiders, the insignificant class of other people. If he could have consulted his own feelings alone, therefore, and had possessed the necessary balance in the Venables' books in the City to enable him so to follow them, he would have remained single all the days of his life, and allowed the title and estates (if any) to descend after his day to his remote second cousin, Owen Llanfyllin Montgomery, of the Inland Revenue.

But there were two cogent reasons which drove the Duke now, while the sod was still fresh on his brother's grave, to run down to Hurst Croft on a strictly business-like errand. In the first place, his credit demanded that he should supply himself at once with ready money, or its equivalent in expectations of a negotiable character. In the second place, his mother, the Dowager, had strongly impressed upon him the absolute necessity of saving what remained of the family property by a judicious matrimonial sacrifice, and of raising up a direct heir of the senior branch to the Dukedom of Powysland.

'Let me see,' the Duchess had said, wiping her red eyes with a dainty cambric, and playing calmly meanwhile with her tortoise-shell quizzing glasses. 'Who is there you could fix upon? There's the daughter of that man who was Lord Mayor last year, of course. She has lots of money, they say, and she's perfectly presentable. She isn't as young as she was, to be sure, but she lights up well, and has good shoulders. She'd cut a very decent figure at a drawing-room still, any day.'

'I dislike her,' the son answered with the undisguised frankness of private life. 'I distinctly object to her. I don't want to pretend to high sentiment and all that sort of thing; but I'd rather not marry a woman who lights up well, and whom I distinctly object to. . . . Unless, of course, it was a matter of absolute necessity.'

The Duchess twirled her glasses slowly round once more in deliberative fingers. 'Then there's that brewer girl, Miss Massy-Smith,' she went on reflectively. 'Old Massy-Smith would pay down handsomely, I haven't the least doubt, to make his daughter a Duchess.'

'What! That red-haired creature!' the Duke ejaculated, with some obvious annoyance. 'Why, I wouldn't take her at any price, mother. I should be ashamed to be seen at Monte Carlo, or anywhere smart, with a woman like that. Besides, she's so fat; they'd say she represented the family stout, and was sent about the country as a sort of living advertisement, don't you know: Before using—and After.'

The Duchess drew herself up, and reflected once more. Her own hair had been generously described as bright auburn in youth, and the seventh Duke had married her from a family not remotely connected with the beer-producing interest; so that her son's remark almost verged on the personal—especially as her own maturer charms distinctly took the direction of a certain chastened massiveness.

'Well, how about that Venables girl?' she asked again. 'She's a fine-built creature, handsome and well made, and clever into the bargain; and Venables père must have nothing on earth to do with his money, dear, stupid old man, except just simply to roll in it!'

The Duke hesitated. 'Well, I like her,' he said. 'I've thought about her more than once. In fact, in a way, she decidedly attracts me. She's a devilish fine girl—there's no denying that. And I admit she amuses me. But do you know, mumsie,' and he hesitated for a second—a Montgomery could hardly make such an avowal without some tinge of hesitation—'I'm not quite sure whether she'd have me if I asked her.'

His mother's face broke into a scornful smile. 'Nonsense, Bertie,' she answered. 'What an absurd idea! The girl would just jump at you. Take my word for that.' For it was her grace's habit to measure all other women by her own individual standard of reference; and she remembered well how hard she and all her family had angled in their day to catch Leopold Augustus, seventh Duke of Powysland.

'Well, but, mother, I've been going there a great deal all through the summer, and half a dozen times over I've been on the very point of proposing to her——

'*Not* proposing, my dear boy. A man in your position never proposes. Offering her your hand—which, of course, she'd snap at.'

'And I've been so discouraged each time by her queer behaviour that I've put it off over and over again; for there's one thing on earth I could never endure, and that would be that a woman should be in the position to say I'd asked her and she'd refused me.'

'No woman alive dare say it!' his mother answered with warmth. 'Besides, no woman's likely to be such a precious fool either.'

'Well, you never know,' the Duke proceeded thoughtfully. 'This is such a queer, proud girl. She behaves so oddly to one. She often seems intentionally to make a man feel she thinks no more of him than of the merest broomstick of a country curate. Why, she's almost positively rude to me sometimes.'

The Duchess smiled. 'That's her way of drawing you on, my dear,' she answered. 'I know the type. And I know the tactics. Not bad tactics, either, for a certain sort of girl, with a certain sort of man. They hold you off with one hand, while they draw you on with the other. But they always mean in the end to take you.'

'*She* doesn't seem to mean it,' Bertie mused to himself, in a serious mood.

'You were only Lord Adalbert Montgomery then,' his mother answered, with a conventional sigh and a faint upward tendency of her dainty pocket-handkerchief, symbolical of maternal desire to check ere it came the rising tear. 'Poor Algernon's death has made a great difference, of course. Not that I think she'd ever have refused you even as Lord Adalbert, and heir-presumptive to the title. But, still, nobody could have expected poor Algernon's life would be cut short like that'—and here the tears actually coursed down the Duchess's cheek unchecked—'so that of course an heir might have been born at any time; and that would have put you in quite a different position. As things stand now, all that's so changed. Take my word for it, Bertie; I know the world I live in, and I know a girl like Sabine Venables—her name's Sabine, isn't it?—would never be such a fool as to throw away for ever one chance in life of making herself a Duchess.'

Bertie hesitated still. 'The fact is,' he

said apologetically, 'I believe she's got a fancy for a man called Harrison, a sort of a penny-a-lining fellow, who writes in the papers. She doesn't talk much to him in public—which is all the more dangerous—but Mrs. Bouverie-Barton says she's awfully gone upon him.'

'Mashed?' the Duchess suggested, with a condescending smile. 'Well, my dear boy, you must surely know *that* doesn't matter twopence. She may be in love with the penny-a-lining fellow who writes for the papers—I dare say she *is* very much in love indeed with him; but love's not everything. If *you* were to ask her, I'd lay a hundred to one in ponies, as soon as look at it, against the penny-a-lining fellow who writes for the papers, and I don't think I'd get any sensible person in England to take me either.' For the Duchess had lived all her life in sporting circles, and this fractional method of calculating chances on a debated event came as naturally to her lips as moral platitudes to Old Affability's.

So, fortified by the Dowager's maternal encouragements, the ninth Duke of Powys-land went down to Hurst Croft only ten days after his brother's death and his own accession to the title, to lay his heart, his hand, and his newly-acquired strawberry-leaves at Sabine Venab ' feet, with very little doubt indeed in his own mind that Sabine would gladly accept the lot at owner's valuation.

The typical English Philistine was at home that afternoon; but he wisely proposed a stroll and tea on the lawn as the best means of leaving the young people alone together. Nature was so beautiful, he observed, and the skylarks were singing. So as they walked through the grounds, Mr. Venables and the companion discreetly in front, intent upon the skylarks, the Duke and Sabine loitering accidentally behind beneath the alley of rose-bushes, the young man found an opportunity in some clumsily sporting way to suggest his errand to the not wholly unprepared ears of the lady of his selection.

Sabine listened to him, as he floundered through his awkward proposal, without moving a muscle of that haughty face of hers. Once or twice, indeed, when the Duke paused and appealed to her mutely to take the rest of a sentence for granted as an assistance to his rhetoric, she smiled internally as she contrasted his clumsiness to herself with Hubert Harrison's ready command of phrase and compliment; but externally, not a curl of the lip, not a flash of the eye, betrayed for one moment her hidden meaning. Cruel in her coquetry, as was her wont by nature, she made the unfortunate young man formulate his ideas in full to the uttermost syllable, without one glance to cut short a hard declaration or to interpret an unfinished and halting sentence. The Duke gazed at her pleadingly, but her face was as enigmatical as a sphinx's and as unmoved as a statue's. Once or twice he paused for breath, and halted nervously. But Sabine just waited till he was ready to go on again, and answered nothing. She would hear it all out in the plainest terms from his own lips, that he offered unreservedly to make her a Duchess.

There should be no mistake or doubt about the absoluteness of the offer. In so many words, he should ask her definitely to marry him. He should have no loophole of retreat left whereby he might pretend he had only put out a casual feeler. It should be a fair and square proposal to make her his wife outright, in sound English phrase, without doubt or condition.

At last, the unhappy young man, his patience exhausted with looking out for some reply, some word of encouragement, some glance of recognition, burst out with a visible effort, 'In short, Miss Venables, I've come down this afternoon to ask you if you'll marry me.'

'Of course,' Sabine answered with a very quiet, matter-of-fact air.

The Duke started. He was prepared for

acquiescence; he expected her, in fact, to jump at him, as his mother had said; but, still, he had hardly looked forward in his wildest moments to such unconventional frankness of acceptance as this. It fairly took his breath away.

'Then you mean to say you answer *Yes?*' he put in, quite tremulously. She was a splendid girl after all, and even Dukes (though the fact is not generally known in England) are really human.

Sabine drew herself up with an astonished air. 'I mean nothing of the sort,' she answered curtly. 'You quite misunderstand me. I said, of course you'd come down this afternoon on purpose to ask me. Anybody could see that the moment you arrived. It was quite evident at once. I was waiting for you to speak and to finish what you had to say before I thought what answer I should give your question. It's always better to hear what the question is, don't you know, before trying to answer it.'

The Duke looked at her with a curious glance, compounded of frank admiration and frank suspicion. 'You're so awfully hard to understand, Miss Venables!' he cried, with a tremor in his throat. 'Perhaps that's one of the things that makes me like you so much. You give one such lots to think about. But you needn't keep a fellow in suspense like this. Remember, your answer means a great deal to me.'

'Not quite so much as you think, perhaps,' Sabine replied with quiet emphasis. 'Before I answer you, Lord Adalbert—I beg your pardon; it's so hard to remember you're a Duke now—but before I answer you, anyhow, I want to tell you something that may perhaps make a considerable difference to you. I mention it in confidence, as it was mentioned to me. . . . My father's going to marry again before long. He's going to marry Woodbine Weatherley.'

'The dickens he is!' the Duke murmured to himself. 'That certainly alters things.'

But he was enough of a gentleman to answer aloud in his chivalrous manner, in spite of this thunderbolt, 'I don't see what difference that can possibly make in my attitude towards you, Sabine.'

He called her Sabine with a little thrill in his voice, and with the pleasant consciousness of performing a very generous action. Contiguity to a beautiful woman counts for much. His heart beat high. At that moment he loved her. He loved her so well, and he thought it so honourable of her to tell him the whole truth before giving him her answer—so as to let him withdraw his offer in time if he were so disposed under these altered circumstances—that he made up his mind at once to a desperate course of quixotic fanaticism. Yes, in spite of everything, he would plunge, and be hanged to it. He determined then and there, as he tried to catch Sabine's hand in his, under cover of the rose-bushes, that, fortune or no fortune, he'd marry that splendid creature, and make a Duchess of her. Besides, who could tell whether Old Affability would ever have a son and heir, after all, or not; and if not, then the young man felt he would have turned out a brick and acted nobly, at no ultimate pecuniary loss to himself in any way.

One must have been brought up in an atmosphere of entail and settlements, and equity of redemption, where to sell one's virility for money seems both natural and praiseworthy, in order to enter fully into the feelings of a man who thinks it rather a magnanimous thing than otherwise to neglect a chance of getting the highest market price for his manhood. So the Duke stood there in all sober seriousness, patting himself on the back mentally for his chivalrous determination not to let a beautiful girl see that the disappearance or eclipse of her prospective fortune had the slightest effect upon his appreciation of her womanly charms; and repeating meanwhile in a very sentimental voice, 'I don't really see what difference that can possibly make in my attitude towards you.'

'But I see what difference it can make in mine,' Sabine answered quietly, her fingers eluding his grasp as she spoke. 'I think in saying *that* you're acting like a gentleman. You don't want me to feel it was my money you proposed for, not myself. And I dare say you proposed to some extent for myself into the bargain. But I won't let you spoil your prospects like that. I know how you people who move in the big world look at these things; and I won't let any man marry me out of a pure momentary access of courtesy. You'd regret it to-morrow, you know. You'd be sorry you spoke to me. Besides,' she added after a pause, with an unexpected outburst of most unflattering frankness, 'to tell you the truth, even before this happened, I'd made up my mind irrevocably to refuse you.'

'To refuse me!' the Duke blurted out, gazing at her and gasping.

'Yes,' Sabine answered, 'to refuse you;

and for a very good reason, too—because I don't care for you.'

'But, my dear Miss Venables——'

'Don't let's say any more, Duke. This is more than enough. I oughtn't to have let you say so much. But I wanted to know, don't you know; I couldn't help waiting till I'd heard you out to the end, to see whether or not you really meant it. Well, I mean what I say. In no case would I marry you. So that's settled once for all. But we may go on in future just as if this little episode had never occurred. My father will ask me what you wanted to say; and I shall tell my father, in strict confidence; but I shall never whisper a word of it to anyone else on earth. Nor will he, either. For that, you have my solemn promise and word of honour. I'm sorry now I allowed you to say so much; but I wouldn't have allowed you if I meant to go away and tell anybody else I'd refused the Duke of Powysland.'

The Duke bowed stiffly. He was quite

taken aback. 'You're very kind,' he faltered out, feeling dimly that he hadn't been quite so magnanimous as he at first imagined. 'I suppose this chapter's really closed between us. But you'll speak of it to nobody then—not even to . . . eh . . . Harrison?' And he glanced at her meaningly.

A red spot burnt in Sabine's cheek once more, but she merely answered, 'I have promised you already. I shall speak of it to *nobody*. And then do you know what all the world will say? All the world has been watching us two for the last six months, and talking about us, and quizzing us, and wondering what it would come to. I knew they were. It's my own fault for trying to play a cruel game. I shall have my punishment. I let it go on too long. I wanted the honour and glory of it. And now all the world will say: She wouldn't have the courtesy lord when she might, and when she'd like the Duke, he doesn't care to take her.'

Adalbert Montgomery felt a pang of pity

for her humbled pride—thus openly confessed —thrill through and through him. 'Sooner than they should say that,' he cried, in another sudden little outburst of chivalrous enthusiasm, this time more genuine, 'I'll have it put about myself at all the clubs that I proposed to you and you rejected me.'

Sabine's eyes had a little dim moisture in them. She didn't care for the young man, yet she was not insensible to the pleasure of holding a Duke thus in leash for a moment. It was the woman now, she knew, and not the heiress. 'No, no,' she answered, trembling. 'I deserve it all. I've told you this because I know I deserve it, and I ought to be punished. I should be ashamed not to take my punishment standing, when it comes, and to submit to it willingly. I ought never to have led you on as I did. I only meant to coquette with you. I coquetted too long. And now this has turned up, and I feel the difference it must make to you and to everybody, and I know I was wrong. Will you think it very strange of me? I want you to forgive me. You do? Yes, then, thank you. And now I think we must go up to the house again to papa. That was really kind. I'm very much obliged to you.'

'Well. He spoke to you at last, Sabine,' the typical British Philistine observed an hour or two later, rubbing his hands in his glee. 'I'm not so blind but I could make that much out for myself. And what did he say to you?'

'He asked me to be his wife, papa.' Sabine responded coldly.

'My darling!' Mr. Venables cried, rushing over and kissing her effusively on both her cheeks. 'I congratulate you! I congratulate you! To think of such an honour! But you're worthy of it, Sabine. Though I say it myself, you're worthy of it. As you stand there this minute, you look every inch a Duchess.'

Sabine disentangled herself calmly from

her father's embrace. 'And I told him,' she went on in a very frigid voice, as if merely continuing her interrupted narrative, 'you were going to marry Woodbine Weatherley, and that under those circumstances it would be impossible for me to dream of accepting his offer.'

'Sabine!'

The wounded Philistine said it in a sudden horror of incredulity and fear. Was the girl going mad? Had she really and truly refused in cold blood the ineffable honour of being made a Duchess?

'Well, papa?'

'You didn't! you couldn't! you can't mean to tell me you actually refused him!'

'Yes, I did, papa. I refused him point-blank. Irrevocably, unconditionally. So that's the whole truth. I couldn't let him marry me on spec. for a fortune. And, besides, what's more, I couldn't possibly love him.'

CHAPTER XIII.

DISILLUSIONED.

Basil Maclaine sat jauntily in his chambers in Clandon Street once more, journal in hand, discussing the affairs of the universe with Douglas Harrison. Breakfast was over, and it was a departmental holiday at the Board of Trade. A man may take his ease at his inn ; and Basil Maclaine took his, by dangling his legs over the arm of his chair, and puffing out successive rings of scented tobacco-smoke.

'Well, it's my belief,' he said with flippant familiarity, 'Powysland's luffed off that tack altogether now ; and the coast's left clear accordingly for a commoner to tackle her.'

'It's my belief,' Douglas Harrison interposed, 'that the Duke, on the contrary, has offered himself and been refused. But as it's no business of ours, we're fortunately not called upon to produce any evidence either way in defence of our opinions.'

'I'm not so sure of that,' Basil Maclaine replied, his eye still resting obliquely upon the paragraph in *Truth* which had aroused the discussion. 'I mean I don't know that it's no business of ours. I don't for a moment believe that she's refused Powysland—not likely she would: girls, even when they're rich, don't often get a chance of refusing a coronet. But I think Powysland must have made it clear to them at Hurst Croft he didn't mean to propose, now he's a Duke—he can do better elsewhere—or else they wouldn't have announced this ridiculous engagement of Old Affability's with that shadowy little Weatherley girl.'

'You think not?' Douglas asked, with a faint smile.

'Oh, I'm sure they wouldn't, my dear fellow! It stands to reason. I was watching that little comedy all through the rehearsals, and I spotted it at once, and so did Mrs. Bouverie-Barton. My only wonder was Miss Venables didn't spot it herself as soon as we did. The old man was gone just silly over dear Woodbine's acting. He hardly ever spoke to me about anything else, except whether Miss Weatherley's dress was the absolutely correctest thing out for the part of Celia; whether Miss Weatherley's points were all properly made; whether every other character in the whole piece was devoting himself or herself with a single mind to the one solitary task of playing up direct to Miss Weatherley as a centre. Depend upon it, it was all arranged between them weeks ago; but they deferred the announcement till Bertie Montgomery, as he was then, had made up his mind to propose or not propose to Sabine Venables.'

'Oh, that's what you make of it, then, is it?' Douglas interjected languidly, for to him this gossip of the boudoirs was by no means so enthralling as to the devoted imitator of the very best models.

'Of course that's it,' Basil went on, delighted with the profundity of his own critical insight. 'You can see the whole thing with half an eye, if you only look close enough. But when Bertie Montgomery found himself suddenly transformed into a real live Duke, he thought better of his intention. Till then, he'd half made up his mind to propose to the girl outright. But the dukedom put him off that tack at once. He luffed and went over. You see, he could sell himself higher in a better market. America's the place now. It's my belief he meant to propose that very afternoon of the pastoral play; but Morton came down with the telegram of his brother's death and spoiled it all. The girl's had a narrow squeak of being made a Duchess, I can tell you, and missed it by exactly twenty minutes.'

It gave Basil Maclaine infinite pleasure thus to feel himself brought into close contact with the high places of the world, and able to criticise such distinguished conduct from a platform of equality. He stood a good half-inch taller now, since he had begun to speak familiarly of a noble Duke as plain Powysland.

'But what did you mean by saying, a minute ago, you didn't know it was no business of ours?' Douglas asked with some curiosity, for he wondered whether Basil was thinking of his brother Hubert. (Life is one long game of these personal cross-purposes.)

Basil Maclaine glanced down approvingly at his own neat walking shoes, as he answered with some magnificence of manner, 'Well, you see, the Duke's clear out of the way, now, that's quite certain. *He* won't marry her on the off chance of the second Mrs. Venables never happening to present Old Affability with a son and heir. You never can count upon an heiress for certain till her father's ninety, or comfortably settled in Kensal Green Cemetery. So, of course, there's a decent chance going at present for any other enterprising young man who'd be content to take a son for granted, and to put up with a modest daughter's share of the Venables millions.'

'But I don't want to marry Sabine Venables,' Douglas responded, somewhat bewildered, for he supposed Basil must still be referring obliquely to his brother Hubert.

'I didn't for one moment suppose you did,' Basil retorted, drawing himself up with one of his superior glances. 'But *I* may. There's your aristocratic insolence coming out again, Harrison. Why shouldn't I have as good a right to have a shot at Miss Venables, and as good a chance of hitting the mark, as any other fellow?'

'Oh, of course,' Douglas answered, with a certain uneasy air of *arrière pensée*.

'Why this mental reservation?' the civil servant put in searchingly.

'Well, it's not my place to speak about it again,' Douglas went on, with some hesitation; 'but do you know, Maclaine, I think, if you mean to marry anybody else, you—excuse my recurring to it—but you oughtn't to go on as you do with Miss Figgins.'

'Miss Figgins!' Basil repeated, with infinite scorn in his voice. 'There you're at it again! What a fellow you are! You seem to think because a man's people are in trade he can't have a particle of self-respect in his composition in any way. That's what comes of having a father engaged in performing archidiaconal functions. Bless your heart, archdeacons and their families are not the only people in the world with any proper pride in them. Now, do you think it likely a man in my position would ruin himself for life by marrying Miss Figgins?'

Douglas Harrison gazed across at him with a curious look of hesitation. 'I can hardly understand you, Maclaine,' he answered after a short pause. 'Long as we've lived together, I can hardly understand you.'

'Well now, look here, my dear fellow,' the civil servant answered, rising, and leaning his arm argumentatively on the mantelpiece. 'What sort of fuss do you think my father and my friends would kick up if I went down to Birmingham and told them I was going to marry—not Sabine Venables, or somebody else in my own position in life—but the girl who waited at table in my chambers in Clandon Street? Just imagine me going back to the paternal roof in the Hagley Road, Edgbaston, and telling the governor I was bringing him home a daughter-in-law to introduce to his friends—from a London lodging-house. Why, my father isn't exactly what you call a passionate man, but hang me if I don't think he'd kick me out of the house the moment I ventured even to suggest or hint the bare possibility of such an alliance.'

'You speak a foreign language to me,' Douglas Harrison answered, closing his eyes dreamily in the vain attempt to realize the frame of mind that could so regard his incomparable Linda.

'Besides,' Basil went on, looking down upon him contemptuously, 'there are my prospects in life; I've got *them* to think about. Controllership of corn returns: there's a post that'd suit me down to the ground, when I've worked my way up to it. Twelve hundred a year and pickings. But even supposing I was fool enough in other ways to wish to marry the girl—which I'm far from being—I have my own prospects in life to consider, of course. She's a very nice girl to flirt with and to pull about——'

Douglas Harrison rose in virtuous indignation. 'You never pulled her about,' he cried angrily. 'You daren't. And you know it. Your words are shameful. No man shall use such language about Miss Figgins in my presence. I won't allow it.'

Basil waved his hand with a gentle deprecatory air. 'Well, you needn't get so warm about it, anyhow,' he answered, smiling.

'She isn't wax. Fingers don't leave marks upon her. Besides, I never said I did. I said she was a nice enough girl for the purpose you decline to let me mention; but as to marrying her, why, the idea's ridiculous. Even supposing, as I say, I chose to make a fool of myself as far as affection is concerned—though, for my part, I'm much more likely to fall in love with a girl in a good position in life than with a London lodging-house keeper—still, it isn't likely I'd want to marry anybody at present, unless she had enough money to keep both of us decently. It'll take me ten years at least to carve out my place in the world in the way I've designed it. When I've done that, I may think of settling down and marrying a penniless girl, if I happen to fancy her; but till then—impossible!'

'A foreign language still!' Douglas answered, shutting his eyes once more. 'So utterly alien to everything I hope, and feel, and think, and believe, that I can't even put myself in your place and realize it. I know it's what the political economists call prudence; but for my part, I call it a much harsher name, and I confess I don't care for it.'

Basil Maclaine lighted another cigar with a spill, and strolled to the door. 'Well, that subject's closed,' he said resolutely. 'We won't discuss it again. I *hate* these bickerings. The fact is, you can't talk about that girl without losing your temper. But one thing's certain. I've made up my mind to so much. I never dreamt in my life of marrying Miss Figgins, and whatever comes, I never will marry her.'

'I think you ought to tell her so, then,' Douglas interposed warmly.

'*I* don't. *You* can, if you like. But I should think she'd be very much surprised indeed to find you thought it necessary to assure her of a fact which must already be obvious to the meanest understanding.'

'It's no use my telling her, Maclaine.

She wouldn't believe me. She ought to hear it from your own lips.'

'Well, she won't, then. That's flat. Why should I spoil my own sport for nothing? She's a very nice young woman to flutter about when one has nothing better on hand to do. But marry her! Nonsense! Why should I tell her I don't mean to propose what in her wildest moments of excitement she could never have expected of me?'

'Maclaine, you're breaking that girl's heart!'

Basil stuck his hat on his head with a very decisive air, and pulled his necktie straight. It rather flattered his soul than otherwise to be treated as a lady-killer, though even on so humble a plane of life. 'Then it's all her own fault,' he answered. 'But she can't be quite such a fool as all that comes to, either. She can never have imagined for half a moment a man in *my* position meant anything serious.'

And he strolled casually to the door, puffing

away at his cigar with an elaborate air of profound decision.

As soon as he was gone, Douglas passed through the folding doors into his own bedroom, which opened out of their joint sitting-room.

The doors were ajar, for the floor was arranged in the common London lodging-house fashion—drawing-room in front, bedroom behind, folding doors between, and a separate door for each room on to the landing.

He entered the bedroom noiselessly, gliding through the open space, not intentionally, but of pure accident, because his movements were always naturally gentle. As he did so, an unexpected sight met his eye.

Linda stood there, transfixed, by the bottom of the bed, leaning on the brass rail of the bedstead for support, deadly pale, and very ghastly to look upon.

'Linda!' the young man cried, his own lips trembling with sympathetic horror.

'You heard what he said, then? Oh, Linda, you heard him!'

Linda put her hand to her side, as if breath failed her. 'I didn't mean to, Mr. Harrison,' she answered. 'I wasn't trying to listen. I'd only just come in to tidy up the room, and caught the tag end of your conversation. When I heard you were talking of me, I tried to slip away without either of you noticing it. But if I'd slipped away, I must have passed the door, and Mr. Maclaine would have seen me in the glass, for he was looking in the glass, and I couldn't have endured that he should know I'd heard what he said of me. It was bad enough he should say it, and that I should overhear him; but that he should know I'd heard, I could never have survived it.'

Douglas Harrison gazed at her fixedly for a moment. 'Linda,' he said, in a very pained voice, 'this is a terrible blow for you; but as he thinks and feels like that, for your own sake, not mine, I'm not sorry you should have found it out at last. I'm not sorry you should know he never meant anything.'

Linda lifted up her face, now scarlet with shame. 'It's all over,' she answered, in heart-broken accents. 'He shall never have the chance of speaking so again. Mr. Harrison, you've always been a dear, kind friend to me. I wish I could have loved you as I have loved that man. But it's all over now. He shall never again be able to say such things of me.'

And, with her head erect and proud once more, but her heart standing still, she walked firmly to the door, which Douglas Harrison held open for her, with a deferential air, as he would have held it open for any other lady.

CHAPTER XIV.

MR. MACLAINE INTERVIEWED.

THAT evening Cecil Figgins came home from the tube-works elastic as usual, full of manifold resolutions for the future. He had made up his mind, in fact, to several important steps. And some of them he intended to carry out, for once in his life, without even so much as consulting Linda.

Douglas Harrison was dining out that night in the West-End, and Basil Maclaine sat alone accordingly, with that blushing journalistic nymph, the *Globe*, to keep him company, in the sacred shades of the drawing-rooms at Clandon Street. Linda had gone to bed betimes; she complained of headache, and seemed sadly out of sorts; but her early disappearance from the scene exactly suited her brother's convenience; for he wanted to talk with Basil Maclaine alone, and this was precisely the opportunity he had long been looking for. So he washed off the tell-tale grime of the works with as great care and attention as if it had been Sunday morning, and, arraying himself in a clean white shirt and neat black coat, like a capable, self-respecting, superior mechanic that he was, knocked, about half-past eight, with somewhat marked assurance, at the door of the drawing-rooms.

'Come in!' Basil Maclaine called out in his second-best manner—the manner he specially reserved for social inferiors of the better grade; for the bell hadn't rung, and he knew, therefore, it was one of the household, not an outside visitor. So he said 'Come in!' with a certain brisk air of gentle command, and Cecil Figgins entered.

'Oh—ah . . . it's you, then, Mr. Figgins,' Basil murmured, looking up somewhat surprised at this sudden apparition of a clean white shirt, but still keeping both his seat and his hold upon the newspaper. 'Do you want anything this evening?'

'Yes, sir,' Cecil answered, walking boldly across the room and standing by the mantel-piece. 'I wanted a few minutes' conversation with you, if you can spare me the time. There's a subject that closely interests us both on which I have something important to say to you.'

'Indeed!' Basil replied, laying down the paper in surprise, and staring hard at his unexpected visitor, but without even a wave of the hand to motion him into a seat. 'What can that be, I wonder?' It was a profound belief of Basil that Linda's brother 'wanted taking down a peg,' and by that precise altitude, accordingly, he desired always to reduce him.

Cecil Figgins, however, was not the sort of man to remain standing in any other man's rooms, no matter whom he might be talking with; so, to Basil's immense astonishment ('Such coolness, don't you know! A mere journeyman mechanic!' as Basil remarked to a friend some days afterwards), he drew himself forward a chair and seated himself confidently full in front of his magnificent lodger.

'Well, I'm thinking of taking some important steps in life,' the engineer began, with the easy frankness of a man who knows and feels sure of his own position (which Basil, for all his fine talk, never really did); 'and before I do so, as they will necessitate my absence from London for a long time, I thought it best to speak to you with regard to my sister.'

'With regard to Miss Figgins!' Basil repeated with an open stare, wondering what this preamble could possibly be leading up to.

'Well, yes; I shall have to leave her alone in the house,' Cecil Figgins went on, without a shade of embarrassment; 'and as that is so, of course, I'd like to know before I leave what her position and prospects will be for the future.'

Basil looked up with his most patronizing air. The man was taking his right cue now; he was touting for his lodgers. 'Oh, Harrison and I are extremely comfortable here,' he said in an affable tone of voice—'extremely comfortable. We couldn't possibly be more so. I understand from Miss Figgins you've a long lease of the house still to run; but you may rely upon it we're neither of us likely to move out, or to want to move out—unless, of course, anything unexpected turns up to unsettle us—as long as Miss Figgins continues to do as well in the future as she has always done in the past for us.'

Cecil smiled in spite of himself, a quiet, self-contained little smile, the very counterpart of Linda's. 'Oh, I didn't mean that,' he said, with an amused air. 'I've no doubt Linda can always let her rooms if she wants to go on letting them. But what I meant was, I should like to know, before leaving London, how Linda's future in life was likely to shape itself, as on that consideration would largely depend the nature of the arrangements I might make as to the lease—and as to my sister herself, in fact.'

'I—ah—I don't quite understand you!' Basil exclaimed, somewhat bewildered by this curious speech. Why on earth should this man Figgins desire to make a confidant of *him*, of all men, about his arrangements as to his sister and his sister's lodging-house!

'Well, of course, it hasn't escaped my notice,' Cecil went on, growing warm, 'that you've been paying my sister a great deal of attention.'

Basil Maclaine let the silver pencil-case on his watch-chain drop from the hand that was idly toying with it, and raised his eyebrows as he repeated slowly, 'Paying—Miss Figgins—a great deal of attention!'

'Yes,' Cecil remarked once more, rather redder in the face than at first. 'That's exactly what I said. A great deal of attention.'

Basil Maclaine stared at him very hard. 'I think,' he replied, with slow deliberation, petrifying him with his glance, 'there must surely be some mistake somewhere.'

'I think so, too,' the engineer retorted, with a quiet smile that resisted petrifaction. 'A very serious mistake, indeed. But it's not too late to rectify it. I say once more, you've been paying a great deal of attention of late to my sister Linda. Now, what do you mean by it?'

'Nothing,' Basil answered, playing nervously with his top coat-button. 'Nothing at all, I assure you. Absolutely nothing.'

Cecil Figgins measured him from head to foot with his eye in undisguised surprise. 'And you dare to tell me so, sir, without one word of apology?' he cried, in a tremulous tone of suppressed anger.

The civil servant shifted one leg from the other uneasily. 'This is so sudden, Mr.

Figgins,' he said with an evident effort—'so totally unexpected.'

'How so?' Cecil answered, his righteous indignation rising higher each moment. 'If you pay a lady obvious attentions, it's natural you should expect her friends and relations to be interested in your meaning, isn't it?'

'But surely, my good sir,' Basil cried, brought to bay at last, and taking refuge in his one unanswerable argument, 'you couldn't seriously suppose a man in *my* position meant to—ah—to actually *marry* your sister!'

The engineer gazed back at him in frank bewilderment. 'Why not?' he asked simply. 'You admit, practically, you have paid her attentions. With what other object on earth could you possibly have paid her them? Have the goodness to explain to me.'

Basil Maclaine hesitated. 'Well, we two were thrown together here in the rooms, you see,' he said, looking down and inspecting his shoes with less complacency than usual, 'and your sister's a person of engaging manners, and an intelligence, I—I must say—well, very much removed above her position in life; and it was natural, under the circumstances, we should talk with one another occasionally on—on various topics; and I may perhaps, at times, have let slip an unguarded word or two more than I intended. But I assure you it never even once, for a moment, crossed my mind that either she or you——'

He broke off short, for Cecil Figgins had risen and was facing him angrily. 'An intelligence very much above her position in life!' the engineer repeated scornfully. 'Why, do you mean to tell me, Mr. Maclaine, you ever considered yourself, or consider yourself now, a person fitted by nature to form a judgment at all upon my sister's intelligence? If you did, I can only tell you you immensely overrate your own critical powers. I should have been sorry indeed if my sister, with her bright, clear mind, were to throw herself away upon such an extremely ordinary young man as you are; though, if it had been her own marked wish, I could, of course, say nothing in opposition to her. But that you should dare to treat her, who is your natural superior, as in any way anything less than at least your equal—such a girl as Linda—why, it's an idea that never so much as one moment occurred to me as lying within the bounds of human possibility.'

Basil reflected for a second; then he asked with a somewhat crestfallen air, 'To what do I owe the honour of this visit? Did Miss Figgins request you to come up and speak to me?'

'Miss Figgins did not,' the engineer answered, in a very decided voice. 'My sister doesn't even know I've come. If she had known what I meant to do, she would certainly not have allowed me to ask you. But at a moment when I had it in my mind to absent myself from home for a very long time, I chose on my own account to take this means of finding out what was most likely to be my sister's future. I'm glad I did. It confirms my purpose. Linda shall no longer be exposed to your insulting advances. I shall take care she knows what sort of man you are who have dared so to treat her. Though I doubt she will ever believe you could be capable of thinking as unworthily as you do think of her.'

'Well, but, Figgins,' Basil began, assuming the defensive once more for a moment, 'just look at it plainly yourself, and consider the attitude. Put yourself in my place, for example. How could you ever suppose a man in my position—in a Government office, and mixing with the Very Best People—would go and ruin his prospects in life by engaging himself to a girl who keeps a lodging-house!'

Cecil Figgins looked him through and through, with unspeakable contempt in his honest dark eyes. 'I should have thought,' he said proudly, stepping back a pace or two, and examining Basil as one examines some singular wild animal, 'that anybody who was privileged to live under the same roof with my sister would have learnt before this to judge her by some higher standard than that purely artificial one. Not what she does, but what she is, marks my sister's position. Mr. Harrison understands that, and treats her as such a woman ought to be treated. But, then—Mr. Harrison is a gentleman. I always knew you didn't understand it, but I never till now suspected how complete was your misunderstanding. The fact is, you and I are placed so far apart in the scale of being, that it's hard for a man like me to realize even your point of view. To me, the realities of life really count for everything; to you, the conventionalities. You've blinded your eyes so long and so persistently to everything really worth noting in the world, that even when you're privileged to live in the same house with such a woman as my sister, you fail to appreciate the importance and rarity of the privilege. No, sir, don't answer me any more. You've said more than enough already. When you talked of my sister as a girl that keeps a lodging-house, you gave me a clue by which to judge your relative standards of worth, and you may be sure I will never again allow her to be insulted by receiving such unworthy advances as yours are. You're too far beneath her.'

And flinging the words full in Basil's face, like so many bullets, he walked out of the room, fiery hot from his colloquy.

At the head of the stairs Linda called out to him. He hurried up to her bedroom-door. She hadn't begun to undress yet, but was sitting on the bed, with her hands on her knees, looking worn and pale, but very resolute.

'I know what you've been doing, Cecil,' she said, raising her eyes to his. 'I could tell by the tones of your two voices. But I wish you had never gone—I knew it all already, dear.'

'You knew it already, Linda?'

'Yes, Cecil. I knew it.'

'But why didn't you tell me, then? How on earth could you let him go on treating you as he did, if you knew it?'

'It was only since this morning,' Linda answered, without flinching or faltering. She was too brave to cry. 'I overheard him by accident talking to Mr. Harrison while I was doing the bedroom. I can't tell you what he said, the words would choke me—but it was enough to make me feel I couldn't stop here any longer. Cecil, I'll go with you. Let us never part. It would degrade me in my own eyes if after this I remained in London.'

Her brother took her hand gently in his, and soothed it like a woman. 'That's right,' he answered, calming down. 'I'm glad you'll come. I knew it would be worse than useless for you to stay. Though I'm really grieved for poor Mr. Harrison.'

'He'll be sorry to lose me,' Linda put in simply.

'He will,' her brother assented with equal frankness. 'Linda, I wish it could have been him instead of the other one.'

'So do I, Cecil. But these things come up their own way in one's heart, and you can neither help them on nor prevent them. They seem almost as irresponsible as the wind that bloweth where it listeth. You can't force them down, my dear, and you can't control them.'

Her brother looked across at her long and sympathetically. But he said nothing. Linda wasn't a girl with whom any man, however near or dear, could venture to condole on such a subject. He drew a long breath. 'He'll miss you terribly,' he said after a pause.

'Who? Mr. Harrison?' Linda asked, looking up and stifling her emotion.

'Yes, Mr. Harrison. For his sake, Linda, I almost wish you were going to stop here.'

'It is for his sake partly,' Linda answered

with a quiet sigh, 'that I think of going away.'

'How so?' her brother asked with some little surprise. 'I don't quite understand you.'

Linda gazed back at him with her frank, fearless face. 'Why, if I stopped here,' she said simply, 'he'd want me to marry him, and I can never love any other man as I've loved this one. Still, I couldn't bear that dear Mr. Harrison should try just, as it were, to make up to me for the loss of the man I love best, but who I always knew wasn't half as good as him. If I lived here long enough, I'd take Mr. Harrison in the end out of pure pity; and I never could bear that such a dear good soul as he should know I only accepted him at last, because a man I loved a thousand times better had never cared for me enough to marry me.'

She said it deliberately, calmly, critically. From any other woman such an avowal as that at such a moment would have sounded strangely hard and curiously calculating. But between those two it was perfectly natural. Brother and sister, cast in the same mould, understood one another without even the necessity for explanation. Cecil knew that Linda esteemed and respected Douglas Harrison so much that some care for his feelings, even in such a crisis as she was then passing through, was perfectly natural to her. For a good woman can like and respect a man to a very high degree without feeling the least little bit in the world that she really loves him.

END OF VOL. I.

BILLING AND SONS, PRINTERS, GUILDFORD.

www.ingramcontent.com/pod-product-compliance
Lightning Source LLC
Chambersburg PA
CBHW032137230426
43672CB00011B/2364
9783337040338